ON

PHILOSOPHY

WADSWORTH PHILOSOPHERS SERIES

ON

PHILOSOPHY

Garrett Thomson
The College of Wooster

THOMSON

WADSWORTH

Australia • Canada • Mexico • Singapore • Spain • United Kingdom • United States

For more information about our
products, contact us at:
Thomson Learning Academic
Resource Center
1-800-423-0563

For permission to use material from
this text, contact us by:
Phone: 1-800-730-2214
Fax: 1-800-731-2215
Web: www.thomsonrights.com

Asia
Thomson Learning
5 Shenton Way #01-01
UIC Building
Singapore 068808

Australia
Nelson Thomson Learning
102 Dodds Street
South Street
South Melbourne, Victoria 3205
Australia

Canada
Nelson Thomson Learning
1120 Birchmount Road
Toronto, Ontario M1K 5G4
Canada

Europe/Middle East/South Africa
Thomson Learning
High Holborn House
50-51 Bedford Row
London WC1R 4LR
United Kingdom

Latin America
Thomson Learning
Seneca, 53
Colonia Polanco
11560 Mexico D.F.
Mexico

Spain
Paraninfo Thomson Learning
Calle/Magallanes, 25
28015 Madrid, Spain

CONTENTS

Preface

There is a man driving on the freeway. His cell-phone rings. His wife asks him in an anxious voice: 'Where are you?' 'I am driving on the freeway,' he replies. She says: 'Please be careful. I heard on the radio just now that there is a lunatic driving on the wrong side of the freeway.' He replies: 'What do you mean only one of them? There are thousands!'

There are two young Buddhist monks who love to smoke cigarettes. They pluck up courage and decide to ask the head-monk for permission to smoke during the long meditation sessions. The first monk enters the office of the head of the monastery. After a few moments, one can hear shouts of anger coming from the office and the young man walks out with a solemn face, shaking his head. The second young monk enters the office. After a few moments, one can hear howls of laughter coming from the office, and the second monk comes out with a happy smile, nodding his head. The first monk is perplexed and asks his friend: 'Why did he give you approval, when he denied me so categorically? What did you ask him?' The second monk replies: 'I only asked him for permission to meditate while I smoke.'

These jokes remind us that sometimes it really matters how we conceive things. Philosophy is the science and art of conceiving things in new ways. Consequently, an introductory book on philosophy should challenge and stimulate its readers to think and sort out issues for themselves.

At the same time, I want to encourage the feeling that we can make progress in philosophy and to combat the cynicism that asserts that we can only stand still or, worse, only go around and around in circles.

I have tried to achieve these two aims by arguing for definite conclusions regarding some of the central problem areas of philosophy, such as the nature of God, perception, the relation between the mind and body, and ethics. In other words, I have tried to engage in philosophical reasoning myself in order to stimulate others to do the same. I hope that, by doing so, I have shown the power and beauty of philosophical thinking and that I have expressed my own love for this rather special activity.

Furthermore, one of the relatively novel features of this work is that I have tried to set out the arguments for its conclusions as syllogisms, so that my readers can dispute them and take issue with my claims. To be clear, you are supposed to challenge my arguments and conclusions. That is a purpose of the book.

An introductory book on philosophy should provide practical guidance as to how to think philosophically. For this reason, I have included one chapter on the nature of philosophy and five appendices on various philosophical skills and attitudes, such as critical thinking, analysis, reading and writing. I have tried to make these guidelines imminently practical and holistic, focusing on both the intellectual and emotive aspects of the philosophical struggle.

I hope that my readers will take the time to relate these practical tips to the body of the text. In other words, the point of this book is not to convince that my conclusions are right, but rather that you should see philosophical thinking in action and learn from that, by comparing how I have proceeded with the advice I give in the appendices. Please learn from what I do rather than from what I say.

In these ways, this book is tailored for introductory and intermediary courses in philosophy and for the general layperson, who wishes to learn how to practice philosophical reasoning.

Several sections of this book reply on parts of other pieces I have written. In parts of Chapters 5 and 6, I have used material from my book *Bacon to Kant*, Waveland Press, 2001. In writing Chapter 7, I have borrowed from material of G. Thomson and P. Turetzky, 'A Simple Guide to the Philosophy of Mind,' in *The Experience of Philosophy*, edited by D. Kolak and R. Martin, Wadsworth, 1995. Some of the material in Chapter 8 can be found, in a different form, in *On the Meaning of Life*, Wadsworth, 2001. Section V of Chapter 10 relies on sections of my earlier book, *Needs*, Routledge, 1984.

I would like to thank Prof. Dan Kolak for his great help in improving this work. I am very grateful to my mother, June Thomson, who read the whole manuscript and helped me improve the quality of the writing. I would like to dedicate this book to my parents.

WADSWORTH PHILOSOPHERS SERIES

ON

PHILOSOPHY

1

Showing What Others Hide

There is a place in Oxford, where certain male professors sunbathe in the nude. For some reason, the place is called Parsons' Pleasure! The old gentlemen of learning can be found there many summer afternoons reading their newspapers by an inlet that leads into the river Thames. It is not a sight to behold for long, as a few young ladies discovered one unfortunate afternoon. These damsels, the young cream of British society, took a wrong turning in their punt and drifted slowly past Parson's pleasure. There was an embarrassingly long moment during which both parties realized what had happened, and then suddenly the professors shouted 'Oh, my God,' grabbed their newspapers and covered their private parts. All of the professors did this, except the professor of philosophy, who covered his face. When the boat had passed, the other professors turned to the philosopher and asked: "My dear chap, why on earth did you cover your face, and not your private parts like the rest of us?" The Professor looked at them dryly, and replied: "My dear colleagues, you have to realize that in the city of Oxford, *I* am recognized by my face!"

Philosophy should be one of the most exciting subjects you can study in today's universities. I say this because, through the practice of philosophy, one can deepen one's understanding and gain a wide overview of different branches of knowledge. One can grasp the nettle of critical questions for oneself. The practice of philosophy requires one to improve one's thinking and critical skills. It should be an exercise of what Woody Allen calls his second favorite organ, the brain. It is demanding and creative but best of all, one can learn from oneself.

To see how this is possible, consider what philosophy is. The standard definitions are 'the love of wisdom,' 'the analysis of concepts,' and 'the attempt to find answers to fundamental questions.' One problem with these definitions is that they are all correct, because each one is incomplete, and none on its own is enough to give us the overall picture. We need a more complete view of philosophy, in order to make sense of the whole and to fit the different pieces together.

Another problem with these explanations is that they leave out the most important aspect of philosophy, which is the practice. The point of studying philosophy is to actually engage in doing it. You may learn what different thinkers of the past have said, but these pieces of information are not likely to stay with you for long. Acquiring such information is not the main point. The issue is to practice your skills, to develop your talents, and to learn how to think both creatively and critically about philosophical questions. The aim is to help your brain stand on its own feet. Philosophy is a process.

The Activity

Above all, it is a human process. Being an independent thinker is a question of attitude and feeling, as much as of reason. To become one, you have to learn self-reflectively from your own thinking. This means going through a process of asking, analyzing, answering and arguing (the four As, as we shall see later) for yourself. Doing this requires knowing when to be patient, when to simplify, how to be creative and destructive.

Of course, it is an essential aspect of philosophy that one engage in it with the help of others. One can practice it by discussing with friends, by reading, and by listening to others. However, you remain on your own, because it is you who must agree or disagree with what other people assert. You are responsible for your understanding and your attitudes towards knowledge.

When we passively learn lots of facts, the information may hit us as something coming from outside. It does not belong to us. However,

4

our understanding of the world and of ourselves is closer to us than our own eyes. We cannot but own it. It frames our view of the world, determining what we do and the opportunities we lose. In this way, we are responsible for our attitude towards our own understanding. Philosophy is a struggle against our prejudices, thinking patterns and feelings. It is not only an intellectual pursuit because it involves the whole human being. You cannot fight old thought patterns and hidden assumptions in yourself without trying to overcome your own feelings and seeking a good relationship with your own comprehension. (For more on these themes, see Appendix one).

The Stages of Philosophy

Very specific definitions of philosophy offer us only fragments of the bigger picture and we have just seen that this bigger portrait needs to be framed as a process. For these reasons, an overall representation of philosophy should include three stages in a process of development.

1. Step One: Asking

In the first stage, the aim is to be confused. Really, the objective is to feel confused, at a loss, baffled and puzzled. Why is this something to attain? Because this is what it is like to confront a question. This is an aim because we look for answers and actively question only when we feel confused. We search best when we feel lost.

In metaphysics, we have to open ourselves to the mysterious nature of things. This may mean uncovering deep assumptions. When we believe that we understand something, we tend to be complacent and forget that we humans are more ignorant and lost than we usually care to admit. Of course, we humans know how to build televisions, and even how make atoms explode. However, this practical knowledge can make us arrogant and forgetful of the strangeness of life. We have acquired incredible know-how this last century, and this technical knowledge can make us feel comfortable, as if the universe were our own cozy living-room. With such a feeling, we may forget that the universe and our very own selves are incomprehensibly bizarre, and becoming accustomed to this is not the same as understanding it. We are used to how things are, but this does not mean we understand them.

Suppose a rabbit materialized in the corner of the room for a few seconds every hour. At first, we would be very puzzled by this odd phenomenon. However, before long, we would be used to the rabbit appearing. We would complain when it came late and, when others express surprise at the phenomenon, we would be blasé about it: 'Oh that! That is just the rabbit effect!' This is a silly example until you replace 'rabbit' with 'pi meson,' a bizarre type of sub-atomic particle. There are many puzzling phenomena in the universe. The simple fact that we exist is one of them. Our self-consciousness is another. To resuscitate our personal quest for understanding, we need to blow away some of our sense of security and rediscover the questioning attitude we had as children. That is not easy, because typically we like the feeling of knowing, and dislike the feeling of being lost.

This same opening-up is necessary in other areas of living. For example, in a corporation, people may need to expose themselves to questions such as 'Why are we in this business anyway? What is it we are doing?' Without such questioning, there cannot be progress in our understanding. These same kinds of questions can be asked about the social institutions and the activities of our own personal lives that we normally take for granted.

Step Two: Analyzing

Most people think that, after questions, should come answers. This can be a terrible error. Whenever one has a difficult question, it is a mistake to rush to answer it straightaway. One had better understand the question first, for otherwise the answer may be no more than a knee-jerk reaction or a superficial blurting of words. In the second stage of philosophy, we try to understand questions without answering them. We try to improve our questions.

This is true not only in academic philosophy, but also in other areas of life. The major part of any deep problem solving is to know what the problem is. It is so in marketing and management, in personal relationships, in scientific inquiry, and in planning a career. In each case, the problem does not come already packaged and labeled, awaiting a suitable reply. We have to first diagnose the problem and find out how to think about it. When the difficulty is: 'How should I look at this problem?' or 'How should I think about it?' then the problem contains philosophy. When the problem is: 'What is the problem?' then it is conceptual. Sometimes, once we reframe the question, the answer can become obvious and easy.

We need to analyze questions for three reasons. First, without understanding the question properly, the significance of the answer may be lost to us. In the *Hitch-Hiker's Guide to the Galaxy*, the beings from the planet X are tired of being bothered by the deep questions of life. They want to be able to get on with their lives of trading. They decide to settle their metaphysical problems once and for all by

6

building a vast computer, called Deep Thought. Deep Thought will provide them with the answer to the fundamental questions: 'What is it all for?' and 'What is the meaning of life?' The computer informs them that it will take him ten thousand years to work out the solution. 'Never mind,' they reply. 'At least, we shall know the definitive answer then.' Ten thousand years pas by and, it is the big day. Finally, Deep Thought will reveal the secret answer to the mystery of life. The crowds are gathered, waiting outside the palace that houses the computer, The head of state goes up to Deep Thought; 'Do you have the answer ready for us?' he asks.

'Yes, I do,' replies the huge machine.

'What is it then?' asks the chief expectantly.

'I am sorry; I cannot tell you.'

'What? Why can't you tell me?' asks the chief nervously.

'Because you will not like the answer,' asserts the computer.

'Never mind that; just give it to me; this is your duty; that is why we built you!' exclaims the chief.

The computer reflects for a moment: 'Alright; I will tell you the answer to the big question but, first, you must promise to not be angry with me, and not to blame me if you do not like the reply.'

The chief replies eagerly: 'Yes; yes. Of course. Please, just tell me. Everyone is waiting.'

'All right,' says the computer in a very reluctant tone, 'the answer is.... 42.'

'What?' screeches the chief, '42! But, how is that possible?'

And now comes the punch-line and the message of this story: the computer says wisely: 'The trouble is you never understood the question in the first place, and so you cannot expect to understand the answer.'

Understanding does not consist in simply having the answer. We can improve our comprehension without knowing the reply. For example, if we had a good map to or outline of the question 'Does God exist?' we might attain understanding of this issue without having a one-word answer.

The second reason why we need to analyze conceptual questions before answering them is that the question may be mistaken. Have you stopped hitting your mother yet? Obviously, you should not reply to that question. If you answer 'yes,' then that means that you were in the habit of beating her. If 'no,' then this means you are still hitting her. Will you pay me back the $1,000 on Friday or on Saturday? Obviously, you should not reply to this request. Both questions contain an implicit assumption: namely that you have a mother whom you used to beat and that you owe me $1,000. These assumptions are incorrect and, in that sense, the questions are incorrect too.

We should not try to answer questions that are based on false assumptions. Perhaps, the question 'What is the meaning of life?' contains mistaken assumptions, as does the question 'What is the color of the number five?' If we can show that it does, then perhaps we can resolve the enigma or puzzlement that leads us to ask it, without providing any reply. Or, alternatively, we can improve the question by cutting out the false assumption and transforming it into something that is easier to answer.

The third reason why we need to analyze before answering is that sometimes several questions masquerade as one. Questions such as, 'What is the meaning of life?' 'Is Euthanasia morally wrong?' and 'What is the relation between the mind and the nervous system?' contain many different queries, all mixed up. They would confuse us less, if we could separate these components and reply to each one in turn. Hence, once again, there is a need for analysis.

Better responses require better questions. Improving questions is a very different process from answering them. We can ask new and better questions only by improving our understanding of the old ones. Much of the work that goes into solving a problem such as 'When is killing morally wrong?' consists in clarifying the question by showing what 'morally wrong' means. Could computers ever think for themselves? Does God exist? Before answering such questions, we have to unpack them and see what they contain.

What is analysis? Any deep and important question puts enormous pressure on key words. For example, consider the claim 'God exists.' What do the terms 'God' and 'exists' mean? God does not exist in the way that the normal objects that we see and touch do. Thus, when we claim that He exists, what do we mean? When we claim or deny that a computer can think, the word 'think' is doing all the work. We have to explain it. Analysis requires identifying and explaining key terms.

Many people are not used to analyzing words, which are like the aspects of our daily landscape that we take for granted and hardly notice. For example, do you know what the word 'procrastinate' means? Of course, it means 'to put off'. You can explain this word that we use infrequently, perhaps only once a month, at the most. Contrast it with the word 'good.' How often do you employ it? Once every thirty minutes? What does the term 'good' mean? This is a difficult question. 'Good' is a word we use often without examining it. However, if, for instance, we want to know what a good life is, then we have to understand how the expression 'good' works. Analysis is the attempt to gain insight by exploring meaning. See Appendix three on analysis.

Analysis points in two directions: back to the question and forward to the answer. Analysis helps us amend the question, and the

8

new question can be analyzed again for more insights. However, this process of analysis should be directed by the need for an answer.

Step 3: Answering and Arguing

We cannot stay at the level of analysis. We also need answers and finding them is the third stage of philosophy. Obviously, not any answer counts as a good one because we want to find answers that are relevant and true. After all, that is the point of beginning the inquiry. This means that, in this third stage, we need to answer and argue.

a) Answering

The answers to philosophical questions do not have to be grandiose theories. They can be simple statements that seem almost obvious once one has completed the analysis. When a philosophical position attempts to solve a range of problems, it is usually called a theory. This reminds us that theories are meant to solve problems and that they do not exist in a vacuum. When considering a theory, it is good to remember this: 'What problems is it supposed to solve?'

b) Arguing

We need to look for evidence or arguments in favor of the theory we are considering, and we also need evidence and arguments against other likely answers. However, more than this, we need to see if there are compelling arguments against the answer that we think is true, which might lead us to change our minds, or at least throw us back into doubt. See appendix two on applying logic.

In the absence of evidence, the best answer would be, 'I do not know.' Without evidence, any theory would be mere speculation, which is only a short step from superstition, a state where people believe things without having any reasons. This is one motivation for critically examining the arguments in favor and against a theory. Without an argument to support it, there is no reason for anyone to believe what you assert.

I am not claiming that philosophy without arguments is useless. A thinker can articulate important insights without arguing for them. However, philosophy without arguments is incomplete and it is an important feature of much philosophy that we should follow the arguments to where they lead us, checking that they are valid as we go along.

What are the Practical Applications?

Perhaps you are wondering what the use of philosophy is, both for you and for society generally. Because philosophy is sometimes very abstract, it seems remote from practical application. I would like to address this concern.

First, theory and practice are not always divorced. Theory concerns our understanding of the world and of ourselves, and understanding usually expresses itself in action. For example, the huge political changes of the last century, which have brought democracy to many nations, depended in part on the development of a theory of rights in earlier centuries. New theories brought new understanding, which gave birth to new actions.

A better grasp of important issues is good news, even if we do not know exactly how we will be usefully employed later. Understanding does not always pay immediate and predictable dividends. The material progress we enjoy now is in part the fruit of the pioneering labor of scientists, mathematicians and philosophers of the 17th century. Our understanding changed, and our actions altered accordingly. The Industrial Revolution was proceeded by a conceptual revolution. None of this was immediate action/result.

Second, the practice of philosophy is an unavoidable part of the human condition, because we cannot avoid conceptual questions, which are an integral part of any area of knowledge, and everyday life. This is because understanding does not consist only in knowing lots of facts. One also has to know how to organize them. The facts have to be framed using concepts.

Third, at a personal level, the practice of philosophy improves our mental capacities. The aim is that, by thinking philosophically, you will enable yourself to reason well: to ask, analyze, answer and argue better.

However, despite all this, philosophy sometimes is remote from practical concerns. In part, this is because philosophers try to concentrate their work on strategic issues and the strategic key point can appear very obtuse without knowing its wider implications. However, academic philosophy sometimes is obtuse and pedantic.

The Nature of the Non-Empirical

Philosophy has three features. We have yet to consider the third.

- The first characteristic of philosophy is that it is a human process of coming to a better understanding.

- The second is that it consists of the three steps. Of these the second, analysis or trying to improve the question, is especially distinctive.
- The third feature is its subject matter, the non-empirical or a priori.

I shall explain this third point in three ways, because it is so important. It is crucial to grasp this point intuitively, as well as intellectually. Without it, we will confuse philosophy with empirical speculation or questions such as 'Do ghosts exist?'

1) First, an empirical question is one that can be settled purely by empirical observation or experimentation. Examples of empirical questions are: 'How many elephants live in Sumatra?' 'What are the characteristics of an electron?' 'What causes cancer?' Such questions are answered by empirical research. However, not all questions are empirical. Examples of non-empirical questions include: 'What is justice?' 'What should count as a good scientific explanation?'

A non-empirical question cannot be settled by empirical evidence alone. This does not mean that empirical evidence is irrelevant, only that it is insufficient Knowledge of the facts is necessary, but not enough. To work in the philosophy of physics, one must have empirical knowledge of physics, but one also must be able to think critically about the concepts used in physics and, for that, empirical knowledge is not enough. To support a non-empirical or a priori truth, a different kind of proof is necessary, namely argument. We try to sustain or refute an a priori claim with a demonstration or an argument.

Consider a detective novel. Suppose that one knows all the relevant clues, but that these are insufficient to answer the question 'Who committed the murder?' To discover the answer, you have to use logical reasoning. You have to know which facts are relevant and be able to make the correct logical deductions, like Sherlock Holmes does. To be clear, the statement 'Jones is the murderer' is obviously empirical. However, the relevant a priori statement, known through deduction, would be something like 'If Henry was in the bedroom at 4.30pm, if Carla was with Frank at 4.30, then the killer had to be Jones.'

2) Here is the second way to think of a priori statements. They are claims such that if they are true, then they are necessarily true. In this sense, statements, such as 'all brothers are males,' cannot not be false. It would be a logical contradiction to deny such a necessary truth. A contradiction is a statement that cannot be true. Consequently, a priori

truths are necessary truths. Here is a preliminary classification of statements:

	NECESSARY	EMPIRICAL
TRUE	2+2=4	Mt. Everest is in Nepal
FALSE	All men are females	London is in Italy

This point relates to the earlier explanation concerning evidence. It is not necessary to gather empirical evidence to support an a priori claim. It would be silly to take out a questionnaire to check whether all brothers are male. You do not have to verify each day whether 2 plus 2 still equals 4. Furthermore, empirical evidence is not enough to support an a priori claim as such. You can interview thousands of brothers to check whether they are all male, but this is not evidence that all brothers *must* be so. To see this, consider mathematics. Mathematics consists of a priori or non-empirical claims. It is not an empirical science and, for this reason, empirical evidence is not sufficient to refute a mathematical claim. Suppose I put two oranges in my magic hat and then another two. Suppose you look inside the hat and there are only three oranges. You would not conclude that, on this occasion, 2 plus 2 equals three. This is because '2 plus 2 equals 4' is a necessary truth. If it is true, it must be true.

We should not confuse necessary truths with claims that we know with certainty. We can be mistaken in thinking that a claim is a necessary truth. People make errors in mathematical calculations! Neither should we think that necessary truths are obvious. They can be difficult to discover. It is possible to ignorant and in with regard to necessary or a priori truths. The point is that we discover such truths by reasoning, not merely by empirical research.

3) The third characterization of a non-empirical or a priori truth consists in an analogy. When one looks at something, one always has to do so through a lens. Without the appropriate lens, one cannot recognize what one perceives. Stone Age man cannot recognize a computer because he doesn't have the concept 'computer.' Without the concept 'friend,' one cannot recognize other people as friends. Concepts are ways of thinking that define how we think, perceive and feel. They are like lenses.

' Let us use this analogy to contrast empirical research and philosophy. Empirical research consists of verifying or falsifying empirical claims about the world through observation. Such observations always require a set of lenses or concepts. We examine

12

the world through a set of lenses. In contrast, in philosophy, we study the lenses rather than the world. We investigate the concepts that we usually look through. Philosophy is the study of concepts. Since understanding often requires reforming concepts, philosophy can be defined as the study of how one should think about a particular area. How can we study concepts? Philosophical investigation requires trying to discover a priori truths that define concepts.

Some Examples

Conceptual questions strike us in all aspects of life. For instance, consider an ordinary empirical inquiry. Suppose we need to make a census to find out how many residents live in a city. However, before beginning any empirical investigation, there are conceptual questions to answer, such as: 'Should we count the people staying in the city only for three months, or the students at the university? To discover how many residents live in the city, one must first answer, 'What is a resident?' This is an a priori or non-empirical question and having a good answer to it is a precondition of the empirical research.

We use concepts in every field of study, and so each has its own philosophical aspect. There is philosophy of biology, physics, art, education, history, literature, sociology, economics, and design. There is the philosophy of architecture, engineering, medicine and development. Philosophy is not restricted to the traditional branches of metaphysics, ethics and epistemology that we shall examine in this book. It is certainly not confined to the study of the history of philosophy. Let us briefly examine some of these areas of philosophy.

1) Psychology:
What is psychology? The standard definition is 'the study of behavior,' but the nature of psychology is conceptually disputed. While many mainstream psychologists think that their work should consist exclusively in conducting controlled behavioral experiments, others deny this. Some affirm, for instance, that psychology should be directed to the causes of behavior, that is mental states and cognitive processes. Other psychologists include unconscious psychological patterns. Others claim that we should investigate the working of the nervous system and others that we should build computer models of cognition. Consequently, there are methodological disputes in the study of psychology, and these are conceptual or philosophical problems, which are not solved experimentally, but rather by conceptual clarification.

2) History:
'What are the causes of the fall of the Roman Empire?' is an empirical question. In contrast, 'What counts as a good historical explanation?' is an a priori question. In the study of history, we look for the reasons that explain, for example, the Reformation, the Industrial Revolution, and the spread of the Inca Empire. However, we also need to answer the non-empirical question: 'What is a historical explanation?' Consider World War II. Should we be thinking of the psychology of leaders such as Hitler or Chamberlain? Or, perhaps, history should concern itself more with the mass of people, or economic forces or the structural features and cultural conditions of nations of the time. Do these different kinds of explanation compete with each other?

3) Biology:
How should we classify species? What is a species? To discover how many species there are in the Amazon basin, one has to know what a species is. Another philosophical question in biology is: 'When can biological facts be explained in terms of purposes?'

4) Economics:
Both micro and macro-economics involve conceptual claims. For example, prices are set at the point at which marginal demand is equal to marginal supply. This is an a priori statement. It gives part of the conceptual framework of micro-economics and defines one aspect of economic rationality. A basic assumption of neo-classical micro-economic theory is that people reveal their preferences with the purchases they make. This is a defining assumption behind the demand curve. Is it true? Can we have preferences that are not expressed in purchases? Furthermore, what is the relationship between consumer preferences and human happiness?

5) Education:
What should children learn? How should a curriculum be defined and set up? In what terms should we define the goals of a university? These are all conceptual questions. To answer them, you have to know about children, schools and universities, but such knowledge is not sufficient to solve these puzzles, which are in part conceptual.

Any field of knowledge has an empirical and a conceptual aspect. Traditionally, the study of science in schools and universities has focused almost exclusively on the empirical aspects of the sciences, such as the experimental method and how to statistically analyze evidence. Rightly, we demand that scientists know how to handle the empirical methods of science with care and courage. But science also has a conceptual side, and this is less often discussed or taught.

Daily Life

We use concepts, such as 'boring,' 'fun,' 'routine,' 'work,' and 'friend,' in our daily lives. Suppose that you are considering what kind of job is best for you, or that you are rethinking your friendship with someone, or that you are reflecting on your obligations as a spouse or as an employee. In each case, you are employing philosophical reasoning. You are probably asking questions, such as 'What is friendship anyway?' and 'What should I be looking for in a job?' Such questions seek the redefinition of key ideas and, as such, they are philosophical because they involve more than the search for information. They also seek better ways to organize or conceptualize what we already know. We all engage in such thinking processes and, thus, we are all philosophers. Not all philosophers live in university philosophy departments.

Business, social and personal problems demand philosophical thinking from us, because actions spring from understanding, which must be framed in terms of ideas or concepts. When we have to examine the relevant conceptual framework, we practice philosophy. Thinkers of any kind need to break the mould of old ways of thinking and reinvent well-worn concepts. Insofar as we all do that, we are all philosophers. Einstein was as much a philosopher of physics as he was a scientist. Jefferson was not only a politician, but also a philosopher of politics. Popular books on personal development, personal health, and business management contain philosophy, because they try to challenge our normal ways of thinking about these areas.

Philosophy is much more than the great metaphysical and ethical questions, such as the meaning of life and the existence of God. This is why there is philosophy of biology, of economics, of business management, of personal growth, of politics, of education, of news media. In any area of knowledge, we use concepts, and the study of those concepts is the philosophy of that branch of knowledge.

Appendix: Beyond Science is not Speculation

Many people place facts and opinions as opposites. Furthermore, they identify facts with scientific facts. As a consequence, they conclude that anything that is not science is merely opinion. Furthermore, they claim that what is merely opinion is purely a matter of subjective taste and conclude that philosophy is purely subjective.

This is an error. Some of the reasons why it is mistaken will be shown in the appendix to Chapter 9. For the moment, suffice it to say that a priori claims are not empirical, but neither are they purely a question of subjective taste. Consider two simple points:

1. First, mathematics is not an empirical science. Yet, it is not purely a matter of taste. One can be ignorant and mistaken in mathematics, because it consists of a priori claims.

2. Second, similarly in philosophy, one can make mistakes and be ignorant. For example, some definitions are better and worse than others, and philosophical theories can be mistaken. Arguments can be unsound. This is because philosophy also consists of a priori claims.

It is sometimes claimed that philosophers disagree with each other about everything. Take any philosophical position and you can find someone who disputes it. Consequently, there is no progress in philosophy.

These claims are mistaken. First, there is actually much more agreement in philosophy than first appears. For example, in the philosophy of mind, some people are dualists and others are materialists. There is disagreement. However, this hides the underlying agreements. A dualist might argue: 'If the private language argument were sound, then materialism would be true, but the argument is not sound.' The materialist might argue: 'If the private language argument were not sound, the dualism would be true, but the argument is sound' (See pages 55 and 78). There is a deep agreement here concerning what the main issue is. Much agreement in philosophy is conditional or qualified in this way. Second, philosophers appear to disagree more than they actually do, because, typically, they focus their work on points of disagreement, usually in the belief that this is the best way to make progress.

2
Arguing about God

Many people cynically assume that there cannot be a sound argument for the existence of God; it is purely a matter of faith. However, this is a big assumption. To be justified in making such a statement, either you know that all the possible arguments for the existence of God are unsound, or have an excellent general a priori reason for thinking that it is impossible to prove such a claim.

One cannot gather evidence for who killed Kennedy by examining the composition of coffee grounds. What counts as proof or evidence for a given fact is not a matter of individual choice or personal belief. What counts as relevant evidence depends in part on the meaning of the proposition and on the relevant causal links. There is no causal chain connecting the murder and the composition of coffee grounds.

Are you sure that there is no proof of God? Perhaps, we can actually show that He exists. We cannot rule out that possibility, without studying the arguments and evidence. We have to examine the best arguments for God, carefully step by step, without prejudice. Moreover, personal belief or faith cannot count as evidence for God, and so we cannot appeal to that to support any position. What's true or false does not depend on one's beliefs. The truth of falsity of the proposition 'God exists' does not depend on what anyone believes, on whether the individual is an atheist, an agnostic or theist. Either God exists or He doesn't - independently of what we happen to believe.

17

Even if the whole world believes that it is false, this does not make it so. Perhaps, there really is a sound argument for the existence of God. Let us look.

The First Move

Perhaps the best evidence for the existence of God is here before our very eyes: the universe itself. Undeniably the universe exists. Whatever it consists of, something exists and the totality of everything that exists is the universe. The more you think about it the more remarkable it is that anything should exist. How can this be? It seems that there are only two possibilities: either it has always existed or it came into being from nothing. Furthermore, if it came into being, then there must be some explanation of this, and the only possible explanation of the universe coming into existence is God. The first argument for the existence of God, which is often called the cosmological argument, is as follows:

1. Something exists
2. If something exists, then there was a first event
3. Everything must have a cause
4. There must be a cause of the first event
5. <u>The only possible cause of the first event is God</u>
6. Therefore, God exists

I have constructed this as a logically valid argument and so the question remains 'Are the premises true?'

Perhaps, the most worrisome of these premises is the second. Let us look at the reasoning in favor of it. The idea is that there must be a first event because it is impossible for the chain of reasons to go on forever. Whatever is happening now must have a cause, which also must have a cause, and so on, but not forever. If the chain of causes extended forever into the past, then that would be like having an infinite number of debts, without there being any money to back them up. In such a case, none of the debts would ever be paid. According to this analogy, an infinite chain of causes would not explain what is happening now, because we always would be left with an explanatory debt on our hands. In an infinite chain of prior causes, any specific cause we single out to explain later events itself must have an earlier cause. Therefore, there is always something remaining to explain. Consequently, there has to be a first event.

This is one way to explain the reasoning that is supposed to support premise 2. Does it actually succeed in justifying premise 2? Its flaw is that relies on an analogy to argue that an infinite chain of causes cannot explain current events. The analogy is weak because it ignores the possibility that prior events are a sufficient explanation of any single event. For example, we can explain event n by citing its cause n-1. Likewise, we can explain event n-1 by citing its cause n-2, and so on. In this way, it can be argued that there is no absurdity to the idea of an infinite chain of past events and, thus, that there is no need to postulate a first event.

To this defenders of the cosmological argument might claim that even if there were an infinite series of past events, there would something to explain, namely why the infinite series as a whole exists and that the only possible cause of this infinite series as a whole is God.

In view of these considerations, perhaps the weakest premise in the above argument is not the second, but the fifth. It has two kinds of problem. First, it seems that God is not a possible cause of the universe. What is the universe? Surely the right definition is everything that exists, and this implies that, if God exists, then He is a part of the universe. In this case, we cannot explain the universe by citing God as its cause, even if He exists. Let us put the point another way: if God exists, then He is part of the universe and, in this case, God is not a possible cause of the universe. A part of the universe cannot be the cause of the whole.

The second problem with premise 5 is that there are other possible causes of the first event, apart from God. Notice that this premise is not: 'The cause of the first event *is* God.' Stated in that way, the premise would beg the question. The sentence 'God caused the first event' already assumes that God exists and, therefore, it presents no independent evidence for the conclusion that He exists. It is a circular argument, which concludes that God exists by assuming that He does.

The fifth premise actually claims that the only *possible* cause of the first event is God and, written in this way, the premise does not make the question begging assumption that He does. Nevertheless, the required term 'only' makes the premise implausible. To refute the fifth premise, we have to show that there are other *possible* causes of the first event, apart from God as traditionally conceived. In fact, there *are* other possible causes of the first event, such as nothingness itself, and Blod, Gog, and Gob. Let me explain. God is traditionally defined as an all-knowing, all-powerful, and all-good being. Blod could be an all-powerful, all-good being that is not all-knowing. Gog is an all-knowing,, all-good being that is not all-powerful, and Gob an all-knowing, all-powerful being that is not all-good. Furthermore, the cause of the first event might not be a being at all. In other words, there is not just one possible cause for the first event and, therefore, this premise is false. Consequently, the argument is not sound and it presents no evidence for the existence of God.

The Second Movement

DNA is an extraordinarily large and complex molecule, and it seems improbable that it could have occurred by pure chance. Looked at in this way, there seems to be plenty of evidence of design in the universe, and the only thing which could design the whole universe is God. The so-called argument from design is that:

1. The Universe has order.
2. If it has order then there must be a design.
3. If there is a design to the universe then there must be a designer.
4. <u>The only possible designer of the universe is God.</u>
5. God exists

Once again, we have constructed this argument so that it is valid and, consequently, to evaluate it, we only have to ask whether the premises are true.

In view of the comments on the fifth premise of the previous argument, we can see that there are other possible designers of the universe apart from God and, therefore, that the argument from design is not sound.

Nevertheless, it is still worth examining the second premise, the reasoning behind which is that the high degree of order we observe in the universe is highly improbable and, therefore, it is almost certainly not just a matter of chance and, thus, it is likely to be designed.

There are two problems with this line of thinking. First, the second premise only offers us two alternative explanations of the order, namely design or chance, when there may be others. Another alternative is that the order in the universe is in part due to physical, causal laws. For example, force equals mass times acceleration. This Newtonian causal law explains much of the order we observe.

Second, his second premise assumes that the order is not due to chance. However, this seems to be an unwarranted claim. Suppose that you have a dice with a trillion sides. You throw it. It comes up on the number 545,678,998,023. You exclaim, 'Goodness me! Do you realize that the probability that it should come up on that number is a trillion to one? This cannot be pure chance.' Of course, it is pure chance, and you would have made the same exclamation whatever number it came up on.

In summary, two of the most interesting arguments for the existence of God fail. Of course, this does not mean that there is not some other argument for God that would succeed. Furthermore, lack of proof does not imply lack of existence.

The Third Movement

In this section, I shall argue that there is good evidence that God, as traditionally defined, does not exist. Here is the argument:

1. If God exists then He is an all-powerful, all-knowing, and all-good being
2. If God exists then there would be no BUNS
3. There is some BUNS.
4. Therefore, God does not exist.

'BUNS' stands for bad or unnecessary suffering. Suffering is bad when there is a conclusive reason to avoid it, and it is unnecessary when it is not required for some purpose of overriding importance. You might think that these are sketchy definitions, but we do not need an overall theory of value to be able to assert that there is some bad or unnecessary suffering. According to what criteria is the suffering bad or unnecessary? We do not require a set of criteria that permits us to place every instance of suffering into the relevant categories: good and bad. It is enough that there is one example of bad or unnecessary suffering.

As I have constructed it, the above is a logically valid argument, and so we must ask whether the premises are true. My strategy shall be to argue that premises 2 and 3 are true, so that if someone wants to defend the claim that God does exist, then he or she must reject the first premise. In other words, I shall be arguing that this argument means that, if we are to claim that God exists, then we have to change the definition of God. We have to conceive of God in a different way.

Premise two is true because if God is all-knowing, then He knows about the bad or unnecessary suffering, if there is any. If He is all-powerful, He could change it. Additionally, if He is all-good, then He would also change it. Consequently, an all-knowing, all-powerful and all-good God would eliminate suffering that is bad or unnecessary, although He would leave good or necessary suffering quite alone. This implies that no actual suffering can be BUNS, if God is all-powerful, knowing and good.

Before examining premise three, I shall answer some objections to premise two.

21

1) EVIL

I have presented the argument in a way that is quite different from how it is normally formulated, in order to avoid irrelevant complications. Specifically, the argument is often stated in terms of evil. I think that evil, which is a theological concept, is beside the point. 'Evil' suggests a malevolent force in the universe and invokes a theological view of ethics. What is at stake in the above argument is something much more simple: the argument states that if there is even one piece of bad or unnecessary suffering, then God does not exist. The argument is not about the place of evil in the universe; rather it concerns whether bad or unnecessary suffering is evidence against the existence of God as normally defined.

2) FREE-WILL

Consider the claim that God cannot exist because there is evil in the world. Some writers answer this by arguing that there is evil because God has given us free-will, and that we have freely chosen to do evil. To this, the atheist reply is that God could have created persons who would have freely chosen to do no (or fewer) evil acts. The theist reply to that is that free-will requires the real possibility of evil. However, this whole debate is irrelevant to the argument I have given, which does not concern the cause of suffering. It is not relevant, for example, whether the cause of BUNS is human stupidity or maliciousness, natural disasters, or even the devil. The argument depends on whether there is any bad or unnecessary suffering, and not on the cause of that suffering. Suppose that you find a person in agony in the street. There is a reason for you to try to stop his or her pain, independently of what the cause of it is. You do not need to allocate blame for that person's suffering. The argument is a question of the existence of BUNS, not its cause.

In defense of the free-will reply, you might claim that God could only eliminate suffering by depriving humans of their free-will. To this I contend that, if the suffering is necessary for the preservation of free-will, then it is not unnecessary suffering. It is needed for free-will, which is indeed precious.

This point takes us to the third premise. Let us compare four sentences:

3:	There is some bad or unnecessary suffering
Not-3:	There is no bad or unnecessary suffering.
IRS1:	Most suffering is good and necessary
IRS2:	All suffering serves some purpose and good

(I have given these statements initials for shorthand purposes. 'IRS' means 'irrelevant statement'). What is it to deny the third premise of our argument, number 3 above? That denial is equivalent to asserting that there is *no* bad or unnecessary suffering. There is not *any*. To deny 3 is to assert Not-3 above, and to demonstrate that Not-3 is false, it is sufficient to present only one case of bad or unnecessary suffering.

Unfortunately, John Hick seems to miss this point in his book, *Evil and the Love of God* (Hick, 1977, p. 253-261). He claims that the argument from suffering fails to show the non-existence of God because suffering is necessary for the development of the soul. Perhaps, Hick is partly right. Perhaps, we have a soul that needs to suffer to develop. However, this is entirely irrelevant to the proceedings. Showing that some, or even most, suffering is good or necessary for spiritual development is not enough to refute the third premise. To refute the premise, we have to show that *no* suffering is bad or unnecessary. In other words, to counter the argument, we have to show Not-3 rather than IRS1. The claim 'Some suffering is good' does not help to establish that there is *no* bad or unnecessary suffering.

Furthermore, to argue for premise 3 and against Not-3, it is sufficient to provide only one example of BUNS. Let us consider one: a baby burning in a fire. I will return to this example in the next section.

Hick also claims that those opposed to his idea are looking for perfect hedonist paradise in which one's every desire is satisfied. This appears to be an argument *ad hominen*, which imputes (allegedly) dishonorable motives to the opponent (see page 154). Of course, if it is such, it does not work, because, even if those people who think that premises 2 and 3 are true are so motivated, this does not mean that premises 2 or 3 are false. In any case, Hick's suggestion is quite incorrect, for it is Hick himself who has to show that this world contains no bad or unnecessary suffering.

You might ask whether suffering is necessarily bad. At the risk of repetition, thinking that this question is relevant is akin to the mistake Hick makes. It is not the issue. I could claim that much of our suffering is good for us because it makes us strong, forward thinking, tough, compassionate, and focused on the more important things in life. All of this could be true and, in which case, suffering in general, ultimately, would be a good thing. However, the third premise says that there is some bad or unnecessary suffering. To deny that premise, you have to show that *no* suffering is bad or unnecessary. The suffering that I need to go through in order to grow is not unnecessary.

Some people claim that everything happens for a reason. They too are trying to deny premise three, without actually succeeding in doing so. Even if everything happens for a reason, the argument against the existence of God is still good. Even if our lives have a purpose, the argument still works. This is because of the simple point that to defeat the argument you have to deny premise 3) and that requires asserting Not-3. The claim that everything happens for a reason does not do that.

4) USEFUL AND NEEDED
To argue that the suffering is necessary, you have to demonstrate that there is no better way to achieve the aim in question. Suppose that you need to learn a lesson, for example, about not leaving your credit card lying around at home when you are away abroad on a long journey. In order to learn this lesson, you become involved in an accident and cannot find a hospital that will take care of you. Finally, a hospital decides to help you, despite the fact that apparently you have no means to pay for your treatment. Through this horrible experience, you learn that it is wise to always carry your credit card with you, in case of an emergency. To claim that the suffering you went through was necessary for the lesson is to assert there was no better way for you to have learned the lesson. Even a fragment less of suffering would not be enough. You have to need it all.

Likewise, when one claims to *need* water, one is asserting that water is the exact thing that one needs. Nothing else can take its place. That is what 'necessary' or 'need' implies. To assert that suffering was necessary implies that one could not have learned the lesson in a more efficient manner. Having reflected on the meaning of these terms, you can see that to claim that *all* suffering is necessary is a very strong and implausible statement. It implies that there is never a better alternative.

These points clarify that, to argue against premise 3, it is not enough to argue for IRS2, namely that all suffering serves some purpose and good. IRS2 merely states that all suffering is useful, but it does not provide evidence for the claim that all suffering is necessary or good (i.e. for Not-3). Something can be useful without being necessary.

5) GOD WOULD NOT ALLOW IT
Some of you may be thinking: 'God is all-perfect, and so the suffering in the world cannot be bad or unnecessary and, consequently, premise 3 is false.' Beware. You cannot assume that an all-powerful, knowing and good God exists to prove that there is no BUNS. The existence of God so defined is what is under dispute. You cannot appeal to that proposition in order to defend it without circularity or begging the question. Compare your idea to the following argument:

1. God exists.
2. Therefore, God exists.

This is a logically valid argument. 'P entails P' is a true sentence. However, the argument is not a good one, because it begs the question, and presents no evidence for the conclusion. The issue at hand is whether God exists. One cannot argue that the third premise is false by asserting that there cannot be any BUNS because God would not allow it. This assumes that God exists and begs the question.

6) ANOTHER MEANING FOR 'GOOD' AND 'BAD'

Another initially tempting idea is that the terms 'good' and 'bad' have one meaning when applied to human actions, and another when applied to God because we cannot apply human standards to God. Effectively, this idea implies that God is amoral or perhaps morally transcendent. A galaxy is amoral because the terms 'morally good' and 'morally bad' do not apply to it and, in this sense, it is beyond human morality. However, if we argue that God is like this, then we are denying premise 1 and this is exactly what I am claiming: that the argument from BUNS implies that, if God exists, then the traditional conception must be false.

7) SOME BAD OR UNNECESSARY SUFFERING

Perhaps, you are ready to bite the bullet, and valiantly try to argue that there is no bad or unnecessary suffering, without fudging the issue. However, without illicitly appealing to the existence of God to support this, it is difficult to see how this proposition can be argued for.

R. Swinburne appears willing do this. In one article, he divides evil into two types: active evil directly caused by the immoral actions of persons, and passive evil caused by natural events and disasters (Swinburne, 1977). He argues that active evil is compatible with the existence of God, because of the free-will defense: God gave persons free-will and this implies that they have the capacity to act immorally. He also argues that passive evil is compatible with the existence of God, because it results from the laws of nature without which there would be no regularity in nature. Apparently, passive evil is the price we must pay for living in a regular, orderly world.

If these points are to be relevant to the denial of premise 3, the upshot of Swinburne's argument must be that there is no bad or unnecessary suffering in the world. His view must be that all examples of active evil are the necessary price of free-will, and all examples of passive evil are the necessary cost of the causal order in the world. In other words, there is no bad or unnecessary suffering. This is ought to be Swinburne's claim if his points are relevant to the argument.

Is premise 3 true? To argue that it is, it is sufficient to show only one example of BUNS. Consider the example of a baby burning in a fire. You may object that this might not be an example of bad or unnecessary suffering. Perhaps, the burning of the baby will achieve some unknown (to us mortals) purpose, which is for the best. In which case, I would have to construct the example with more care. Suppose, no one knows about this terrible incident, and that, therefore, there can be no question of this event inspiring someone else to prevent further much worse suffering later on. In reply, you might claim that, perhaps, if the baby had lived, he or she would have caused more suffering, and that, after all, this is not an instance of bad or unnecessary suffering. Again, I amend the example to take your point into account. The discussion continues. Suppose I cite another example. Again, you reply that this might not be an example of bad or unnecessary suffering, for reasons unknown to us (see, for example, Alston, 1991).

Such a discussion misses an important point. To show that premise 3 is true, it is *sufficient* to provide only one example of bad and unnecessary suffering. However, that does not mean that it is *necessary* to provide such an example. Perhaps, none of the specific examples I could give would be clear and indisputable instances of BUNS. However, there might be other reasons for thinking that, even if every putative example can be contested, there is some such suffering.

Even if each individual example can be contested with some force or plausibility, this does not mean that all putative examples as a collection can be. It is one thing to claim of any particular example: 'This might not be an instance of BUNS.' It is quite another to claim of all examples together: 'It could be that none of these is an instance of BUNS.' Whereas the first appears reasonable, the second is less so.

There is a good reason for thinking that premise 3 is true. To assert Not-3 is to claim that there is never a conclusive reason for preventing suffering. If there is never such a conclusive reason, then what is the point of practical reasoning? In reasoning practically, we try to work out, in conditions of ignorance and uncertainty, what is the best thing to do in the circumstances. We try to discover what we have conclusive reason to do in particular situations. Of course, conclusive reasons are not restricted to simply preventing BUNS. For instance, on occasions, we may have a conclusive reason to not deprive other people of their autonomy by, for instance, jailing them without reason. Nevertheless, if Not-3 were true, then there would never be a conclusive reason for us to prevent and avoid suffering and practical reasoning would be devoid of an important part of its point. It is inadequate to reply to this argument that God knows better, as Swinburne appears to do. For such a rejoinder begs the question and it implies that, if we knew better, then we too would see (just as God allegedly does) that there is never a conclusive reason to avoid suffering.

3

Non-Traditional Conceptions of God

Recently there has been a heated debate about the existence of Slobivech. Despite all the public opinion, the simple question remains: 'Do you believe that Slobivech exists?' Of course, you cannot answer the question unless you know what Slobivech is. This means that, if you think you can answer the question 'Does God exist?' then you must claim to know what God is. We saw in Chapter 2 that the traditional definition of God as an all-perfect being cannot be right, if He exists.

The aim in this chapter is to start again. Instead of concentrating on 'Does God exist?' we should answer the question 'What is God?' In the previous chapter, we jumped from stage one in philosophy to stage three, ignoring the second stage of analysis. Since God cannot be conceived in the traditional way, as an all-perfect being, we need this second stage. Before asking 'Does God exist?' we should carefully examine the question 'What is God?'

Much philosophy of religion assumes a Christian perspective, and even ignores branches within that tradition such as Gnostic thought (B.Layton, 1987). We tend to assume that God is an all-perfect being, separate from the universe that He created. This assumed definition prevents us from better understanding the issues because it initiates the discussion of whether God exists without first properly investigating what God is. In this way, it tends to confuse the defense or critique of a religious tradition with the philosophical investigation of the nature of God. The philosophy of God need not be the philosophy of religion.

Religions are socio-cultural institutions and practices that have developed historically, but thought about God need not be wedded to any one of those institutions. We should not confuse the acceptance of a religion with the belief in God. In other words, we should not uncritically assume that the standard Christian definition of God is correct. Furthermore, the traditional approach fails to answer an important need. Many people sense that there is something important to the concept of God, and yet they feel uneasy with the specifics of the concept as traditionally conceived.

There are many competing conceptions of God, but if they are of the same thing, then we should try to find what they have in common. This means that we have to be less specific than the traditional conception is. This would have the advantage of offering a definition that is culturally more encompassing. For example, we might initially define 'God' as the divine or holy. Alternatively, we could define 'God' as that which we should worship. These two definitions are equivalent, given the assumption that we should worship only something holy or divine. This leaves us with the thorny problems of what divine, holy and worship are, and what could possibly substantiate these properties.

Why is God Important?

Why does it matter whether God exists or not? This is a point concerning which confusion is easy. For example, some people claim that, without God, morality would be impossible; if God does not exist, one might as well go out and steal. This view reduces morality to either a form of self-interest or to a set of authoritarian commands. In the first case, it requires asserting that it is wrong for me to hurt other people only because I will be punished by God. In other words, only my hurt matters. This distorts the nature of morality. Would Mother Teresa have said: 'I do not care about the poor, and all my work is dedicated to help me escape the eternal punishment of God?' The answer is 'no' because it is part and parcel of morality that other people's interests matter. I should not hurt others because their interests count. Therefore, morality does not depend on God giving out punishments.

Coming now to the second case, the idea of right or wrong is independent of what God commands. It is wrong for me to push your hand into the fire simply because it would hurt you. The reason I have to not place my own hand in the fire is the same as the reason for not putting yours there, namely the avoidance of pain. This explanation of its being wrong renders morality independent of the existence and

28

commands of God. In Chapter 9, we shall examine other arguments for the claim that morality does not consist in God's commands.

The existence of God might be important in that it helps one feel less insecure. Life is brief and often painful, and death is an unknown. There may be something right about this idea, but it is easy to state the point incorrectly. Let us examine the confused way to put the idea first. According to this, we need belief in God to help us feel more secure. The problem with this idea is that, if it were correct, then it would not matter whether God exists or not. Rather, what would matter is whether one believes in God. According to the idea, it is not God's actual existence that functions like a psychological comforter, but rather the individual's belief in Him. In this way, we have missed the main issue, namely why God's existence matters.

Furthermore, the statement 'I believe in God because it makes me feel secure' is confused because it turns belief into a pill or medicine, rather than an attempt to find out what is true. Perhaps, it would be wiser to face the insecurities of life and death, instead of trying to shape one's beliefs to one's own needs rather than to reality.

This was the wrong way to put the original idea. Let us briefly examine at what might be a more correct way. Life is brief and often painful, and death is an unknown. If God exists, then we might be justified in an attitude of feeling safe, despite these facts. In this way, perhaps, we would be more justified in feeling at home in the universe if God exists. This does not give us reason for thinking that God really does exist, but it might be a relevant interest in defining what God is. Nevertheless, this approach omits something important, the idea of the divine. Perhaps, the core to the idea of God is that of something holy and sacred, such that the only appropriate response is to it is worship.

Section I: God as Transcendent

Suppose I asked 'What color is God? Is He red or, perhaps, green?' Obviously God is not like that. Suppose one answered: 'I do not know.' This would be a mistake, because one would imply that God does have a color, and that one does not know which one. Also, the answer 'God has no color' would be a mistake too because it accepts the question as legitimate. To such an answer, I could reply: 'You mean that He is transparent, like glass, water and air?' That is not right either.

Perhaps, we could write a list of predicate terms that do not apply at all to God. For example, this list would include the terms 'tall' and 'short,' 'hot,' and 'cold,' and 'late' and 'early'. In such cases, neither 'F' nor 'not F' applies to God.

Pairs of words, or families of expressions, imply an implicit warning that cautions: 'Only apply these words within these limits or contexts.' Predicates, such as 'is square,' apply to things within certain limitations. For instance, color words only apply to things that can reflect light. Expressions such as 'tall' and 'short' only apply to objects that can be in space. Thinking seriously about the nature of God requires a struggle with the limits of words.

Normally, we assume that any word that is meaningful must be meaningful in any grammatical sentence in which it occurs. However, this idea is incorrect if predicate expressions have built-in limitations beyond which they do not have meaning. In which case, we can think that a word is meaningful, and yet be mistaken about it. Let us apply this point to the concept 'God.'

Most people approach the question 'Docs God exist?' within the usual categories of theist, atheist and agnostic. An atheist is a person who believes that God does not exist; a theist believes that God does exist, and an agnostic is someone who professes no belief, or who suspends judgment. However, these are not the only categories. Consider the table below.

	1) God	2) 'God'
a) Yes	Theist	
b) No	Atheist	
c) Maybe	Agnostic	

Instead of the usual three categories, there are at least six. Boxes 1a), 1b) and 1c) form the three traditional views of God's existence. In addition, there are boxes 2a), 2b) and 2c), which concern the concept of God and form answers to the question 'Is the concept of God meaningful?' For example, persons in the category 2a) believe that the concept has a meaning that they know or understand. Those in box 2b) claim that the concept has no real sense. Those in the category 2c) claim that the concept may have a meaning, but that, if it does, they do not know what it is. According to this idea, 'God' is a name that designates something that we do not understand.

Positions 1a), 1b) and 1c) have something in common. They assume position 2 a). The atheist who says it is clear there is no God assumes, like the theist and agnostic, that the word 'God' has a meaning that we know and understand. Positions 2b) and 2c) reject this assumption.

30

To see how words that we think have meaning can fail to have meaning, and to better understand position 2b), consider the following example. A nelephant is an invisible, intangible, and utterly undetectable elephant. Given this definition, suppose I claim: 'There are six nelephants in this room.' One might fall into misguided ways of responding to my statement, for example, by arguing: 'You are wrong, and you have no evidence for your claim. There are no nelephants in this room.' This seems like an innocuous, and indeed a true thought. However, beware. If you assert that, then I will reply to you as follows: 'Ah! You think that there are no nelephants in this room. And you complain that my view has no evidence in favor of it! You have no evidence for the claim that there are no nelephants in the room. Your view is without support too. Evidentially speaking, it is no better than mine is. If my view is unfounded, then so is yours.'

This does not seem to be quite right. You wanted to defend commonsense and ended up defeated, with no evidence to support your claim. You have landed yourself in a position, which with a little thought appears as ludicrous as mine.

The problem is that you fought the battle on the wrong ground. This should not be a contest of six versus none, but instead a debate about whether the concept 'nelephant' really has any sense. It is not an issue of knowledge and evidence for and against. The relevant question is: 'Does the concept of a nelephant make sense?' In a way, it does not, as we shall see. This qualification 'in a way' is important, because you understood my original definition of the term, and you have followed the argument up to now and, consequently, the term 'nelephant' does have some meaning. Despite these qualifications, the reply to my claim that there are six nelephants in the room should be: 'Your sentence lacks sense.' In this way, you don't fall into the trap of affirming that there are no nelephants in the room. Instead of disputing the truth of my claim, you should challenge the concept of nelephant.

What is wrong with the statements 'There are six nelephants in the room' and 'There are none?' Words and phrases have built-in presuppositions, which determine their range of applicability. For example, as we have seen, color words have the limitation or presupposition that they apply only to things which can reflect light. Therefore, it does not make sense to assert or deny that gravity is red. 'Gravity is red' carries the implication that gravity is not green, blue or any other color. On the other hand, 'gravity is not red' carries the implication that it should be one of the other colors, such as white, green, blue, yellow, orange, and so on. None of these implications are correct regarding gravity and, consequently, we should not assert or deny the sentence 'Gravity is red.' Although the sentence is meaningful in the sense that it is grammatical, it is devoid of sense, precisely

31

because it violates a condition for the applicability of color words, namely 'Use only in application to things which can reflect light.' The claim that there are no nelephants in the room is similar. Words for material objects carry the assumption that these objects are not undetectable, that they can have causal effects on other things. The concept of nelephant violates that condition.

I have not argued that the concept of God actually is like that of an nelephant. Rather, I have used the example to explain position 2b), to show you how someone who thinks that the concept of God is senseless might argue. To see how we might escape box 2b, please read on.

Beyond Existence

Let us examine the phrases 'God exists' and 'God does not exist.' As we have seen, expressions have a set of built-in presuppositions that delineate their applicability, their range of meaningful application. Consequently, the verb 'exist' should also have conditions of application.

Some thinkers claim that the verb 'exist' can be applied only to things or objects that can be in space and time. Given this analysis, it makes sense to deny that unicorns, green swans and mermaids exist, because they are the kinds of things that could exist in space and time, but actually don't. This analysis would imply that the pair of terms 'exists' and 'does not exist' cannot be applied to God, on almost every conception of God.

However, this analysis of 'exists' is too simplistic, because perhaps some non-spatio-temporal entities can exist, such as sets and numbers. Furthermore, the whole universe itself is not an object in space-time, because it includes all space-time, and so this analysis would imply that we cannot affirm or deny that the universe exists. These are contentious and difficult waters, so let us move on.

If spatio-temporal position is not a presupposition of 'exists,' then what is? One suggestion is that to be is to be the subject of a set of predicates or property-terms. For instance, I exist because I am a human and I am not a river. I exist because a range of property terms applies to me and others do not. Leaving aside the problem of fictional items, such as Batman, this answer would imply that to be is to be something rather than something else. To be is to be limited. Following on from these ideas, Harvard philosopher Robert Nozick tries to explain the concept of the Unlimited or Absolute, that which has no limits at all, or the all-encompassing and all-inclusive (Nozick, pp. 600-3). Nozick notes that, given this view of existence, the Absolute 'would transcend the pair 'existent'/'non-existent,' not satisfying its presuppositions.' We might claim: the Absolute transcends 'existence.'

Some conceptions of God imply that we cannot assert or deny the existence of God, especially if the concept of God is like that of the Absolute. This is quite different from saying that we do not know whether God exists or not. The point is that terms 'exist' and 'does not exist' do not even apply to God.

This does not mean that the concept of God is senseless and should be rejected. It does not imply thinking that box 2b) is the correct one. It does not necessarily put it on a par with the concept of a nelephant. We might argue for the affirmation that the Absolute transcends 'existence,' without thinking that a similar argument would apply to the claim 'nelephants transcend 'existence.'"

To see why, consider briefly an interpretation of part of the philosophy of Kant (1724–1804). Kant believed that objects in space and time are real; they exist independently of being perceived by us. A tree exists whether we perceive it or not. Yet, at the same time, he argued that such objects are transcendentally ideal in the sense that their nature is relative to the necessary conditions of any possible experience, which are the categories and space and time (Thomson, 1992 and 2001). Objects are not relative to us humans, for we too are part of the natural and transcendentally ideal world. They exist without us. Nevertheless, they are relative to the necessary conditions of experience.

In asserting that spatio-temporal objects are transcendentally ideal, Kant meant to deny that they are absolute and, for this reason, he contrasts things in the spatio-temporal world, which he calls phenomenal, with an absolute conception of reality, which he calls noumenal. Kant claimed that the notion of noumena is an empty limiting concept (Kant, 1929, A255-57). Noumena are not objects, but the term stands for the notion of reality not relative to the conditions necessary for any possible experience. This implies that noumena cannot possibly be experienced, or described with the terms we use to characterize objects.

Notice that, according to this interpretation, Kant was not asserting that there are two worlds: the one we know, comprised of things in space and time, and the other, consisting of unknowable noumena. Rather Kant affirmed that there is only one world, which we can know and meaningfully describe only within the parameters of the necessary conditions of possible experience. That same world considered absolutely (as noumena), without those parameters, cannot be meaningfully described.

Among the necessary conditions of possible experience are what Kant calls the categories, which include that of actuality, which we may read as 'existence' (Kant, 1929, A225). The categories only have meaningful application to natural objects in space and time. They have no meaning except in application to things that can be experienced, namely objects in space and time. This implies that the concept of existence cannot be applied to noumena. Therefore, according to this interpretation of Kant, we cannot meaningfully assert or deny that noumena exist. (However, Kant himself does not explicitly draw this conclusion).

The main point is as follows. It would be a travesty of Kant's thought to claim that the notion of noumena was equivalent to that of a nelephant, entirely senseless and without function (although we cannot exclude that a critical analysis of his position would lead us to that conclusion). It would be fairer to claim that Kant thought that noumena transcend 'existence.' For Kant, noumena lie at the limit of thought. We need that empty limiting notion to remind us that real objects in space and time are transcendentally ideal, that is relative to the necessary conditions of any possible experience. Noumena prescribe the limits of thought. In a way, Kant's position is that there is more to the nature of the world than we can even think. According to Kant, this last claim is something we can know to be true, because it is a requirement of science and mathematics. According to Kant, science and mathematics involve non-analytic necessary (or synthetic a priori) truths. To explain how such truths are possible requires the idea that experience has necessary conditions and the truth of Transcendental Idealism (or the phenomenal/noumenal distinction). In other words, science points to the limits of thought and, thereby, beyond to noumena or to the Absolute. In brief, the point of this discussion of Kant is to show that the claim that God transcends the pair of terms 'exists' and 'does not exist' does not automatically mean that the concept of God is senseless.

This aside concerning Kant's idea of noumena is important if there is an affinity between it and God, or what Hick calls the transcendent Reality and Ninian Smart calls the religious ultimate (Hick, 1993, p.28 and Smart, 1979, Ch.2). It is important because it shows that there may be reasons that point towards what cannot be thought or said (even though any attempt to assert what cannot be said will obviously either lead to contradiction or be without sense). This pointing provides a reason for denying that the concept of noumena is similar to that of a nelephant and for asserting that noumena are beyond 'existence,' while nelephants are not. Kant thought there is a God, but he also believed that you cannot even think that, because the words 'exist' and 'is' are tied to the necessary conditions of possible experience, such as space and time. By definition God is beyond these conditions of experience. Consequently, according to a Kantian position, whereas 'nelephant' would belong in box 2b, the concept of 'noumena' belongs in box 2c).

The Inexpressible

Many mystics paradoxically express their experience of the divine as something inexpressible. For example, George Fox wrote 'All the creation gave another smell unto me than before, beyond what words can utter' (Hick, 1993, p.24). The *Kena Upanishad* describes God (Brahman) in this way: 'What cannot be spoken with words, but that thereby words are spoken: know that alone to be Brahman, the Spirit' (Juan Macaró, 1965, p.51).

Morcover, there are reasons for thinking that there is something right about this idea. If God is not a part of this world, then He transcends it and, in this case, we should not expect Him to be describable with concepts born and formed by our experience in this world. If God is transcendent, then He is beyond our (normal) concepts. This view renders God similar to the Kantian notion of noumena.

All religious traditions face this problem of, on the one hand, characterizing God in terms that people can understand and, yet, on the other hand, recognizing that this is in some sense a violation of the real nature of God. For example, consider the claim that one is not supposed to represent God as an idol. Religious traditions want us to able to think about God and, at the same time, they claim that God is beyond understanding. This is paradoxical. However, any deep religious tradition should recognize this dichotomy.

Consider the Old Testament. On the one hand, God is portrayed as a person who gives Moses a message, toys with the Egyptians, and chases them into the sea. On the other hand, there is quite a different idea. The Old Testament describes God as 'I am that I am.' This is like affirming God is the isness of what is. This is very different from claiming that God is a supernatural person who performed the following actions: He punished the Egyptians, led Moses into the wilderness and so on. The same tension exists in the Islamic tradition. On the one hand, God instructs the archangel Gabriel who taught Mohammed. This implies that God is a teacher. On the other hand, the *Koran* also says that God is beyond all distinctions. If God is beyond all distinctions, then He is indescribable.

The claim that God is indescribable is highly problematic, for two important reasons. First, the predicate 'is indescribable' is essentially paradoxical. It is itself a description and, therefore, when it is true of something, it is also false. If God is beyond our concepts, then He is not beyond the concept 'being beyond our concepts.' In a similar way,

Kant's position regarding noumena is paradoxical, and appears contradictory. For instance, the claim that we cannot think about noumena is supposed to be a thought and, therefore if it is true, it is false. It appears that to prescribe the limits of thought, Kant has to go beyond them and, thereby, contradict himself.

There is possible a way out of these problems, even though it requires a fundamental revision to Kant's ideas. We should not claim that noumena are indescribable, full stop, because this is a contradictory notion. Instead, we should specify ways in which the noumenal is indescribable. For instance, noumena cannot be described with the pair 'big'/'small' because they are not spatio-temporal, but this means that they can be described with the predicate 'are not spatio-temporal.' They can also be described with the predicates 'are not subject to the categories' and 'are beyond the conditions of possible experience.'

According to this idea, we should adopt a similar strategy towards the supposed ineffability of God. For example, God cannot be described with the pair 'bald'/'hairy,' but possibly can be described as divine, and as 'is describable neither as 'hairy' nor 'bald.'' In other words, we should reject the blanket and contradictory notion of absolute ineffability, and instead employ the notion of relative ineffability, arguing piece-meal, case by case. For example, God is beyond the distinctions hot and cold, tall and short, and fat and thin.

The second problem is that, even if this strategy works, why should the concept of God as the transcendent have spiritual or broadly religious significance? Remember that earlier we suggested that God could be defined as the divine and that this implies that our attitude towards God should be one of worship. This definition gives the existence of God practical implications for our lives. But what practical significance could the conception of God as the transcendent have?

However, the possibility of pointing towards the transcendent may have practical implications. First, it implies that existence is a mystery because thought has limits. Living in a world that is ultimately mysterious arguably ought to be very different from a world that has nothing more than the features ascribed by physical science. Secondly, Kantian thought has another dimension. Because the noumenal and the phenomenal world are one and the same, in a way we do know the noumenal, but never as such, but only as the phenomenal. On this basis, we might claim, as Kant does, that the phenomenal is an expression of the noumenal (Kant, 1988, p.209-211). If God is noumenal, then the natural world is like a painting that expresses God. In summary, in this section, I have tried to explain the meaning of the idea that God is indescribable or transcendent, and indicate some of the problems inherent in this idea.

Section II: a Dualism: Universe/God

This last point (i.e. that the natural world might be an expression of God) takes us onto another road. Consider the claim that God created the universe. What is the universe? By definition, it is everything that exists. This definition implies that if God exists, then He must be a part of the universe. This entails that we cannot legitimately oppose God and the universe.

Even if we divide the universe into two parts, God and the rest, and even if we assume that only God is divine, we are still left with the question 'What caused the universe?' Also, we are still left with the point that God is part of the universe. If the universe is everything, then no God/ Universe duality is possible. We could redefine 'universe' to signify 'everything except God,' but without a justification, this is a verbal maneuver that leaves the point untouched. A possible justification is that God transcends the universe, but that is the course we explored in the previous section.

In the seventeenth century, Spinoza (1632–1677) realized that there were problems for Descartes' mind/body dualism (Spinoza, 1955). Descartes argued that the mind is a non-material, non-spatial substance, which affected and was causally affected by inert matter in space, in particular the brain (see Chapter 6 below). Spinoza claimed that Descartes' conception of the mind-body relation made causal interaction between the two impossible. How can two substances so unlike causally interact? According to Spinoza, they cannot, for they have nothing in common. Spinoza concluded that Descartes' conception of the mind-body relation (as two entirely different kinds of substances) is mistaken. He used this conclusion to support his claim that there can only be one substance, which he called God or Nature.

Spinoza claimed that the mind and the body, instead of being two different substances, are two aspects of one substance. This double aspect theory enables one to maintain some of the benefits of dualism, without its ontological problems. According to Spinoza's position, one does not have to maintain that the mind is reducible to the body, as a strict materialist might, because the mind and body are two irreducible aspects of one thing. Yet, one could avoid the problems inherent in ontological dualism concerning the interaction between two radically different kinds of substances. Although Spinoza's account of the mind-body relation is fraught with problems, it is a very suggestive theory. (For some of the problems, see Thomson, 2001(b) Chapters 4 & 5).

37

Non-Traditional Conceptions of God

In particular, it suggests an alternative approach to the God/ universe distinction. Indeed, Spinoza realized that the problems of Descartes' mind/body dualism also apply to the cosmic dualism, God/universe. For this reason, Spinoza tried to develop an argument to show that the universe is God. What is fascinating about Spinoza's position is not so much the details of his argument, but his claim that the universe itself has divine qualities. Implicit in his work is a dual-aspect theory of the relationship between the universe and God. Viewed one way the universe is a physical system; viewed in the other, it is something divine. As it were, the universe is God's body.

Spinoza identified God with the whole universe. Perhaps though, it is an error to think of God as a substance at all. Instead we might claim that God is a property of the universe. In which case, God would be the divine aspect or face of the universe.

In much philosophy of religion, the phrase 'divine properties' refers to the traditionally conceived perfect qualities of God, namely omniscience, omnipotence, and moral perfection. However, this view appears to take us back to the traditional idea of God that was rejected in Chapter 2. As an alternative, we could think of 'divine' as whatever warrants an attitude or response of love, awe and worship, such as the qualities of being beautiful, holy, and sacred. Under this interpretation of the Spinoza-like idea, 'God exists' becomes equivalent to 'the nature of the universe is such that it warrants such moral and aesthetic responses or attitudes.' Whether this claim could conceivably be true is a question I shall leave aside. Though, it is worth noting that Wittgenstein thought the universe was worthy of awe, simply for the very fact that it exists (Wittgenstein, 1998, proposition 6.45). Note that, for Spinoza, the divine qualities of the universe that warrant us calling it God, are that it is infinite, self-caused and unique.

Section III: Is God a Being?

The two non-traditional conceptions of God we have considered are very different from the standard conception of God as an all-perfect being. They differ in not treating God as a person or being at all. It is anthropomorphic to describe a car as a person, or to ascribe person-like qualities to something that cannot have such properties, for example, to describe an ant as thoughtful, a buttercup as lazy and a galaxy as bored. We tend to personify God and to conceive the relation between humans and God as similar to the relations between people. There is a tendency to think of God as a father or mother, or as a king or queen. Is it anthropomorphic to conceive of God as a person?

38

Compare this to the status of sub-atomic particles, such as photons, quarks, and pi mesons. Thinking of God as a person may be similar to treating photons as material objects. In most circumstances, photons behave in ways that are more like waves than objects. For example, they do not have a specific location, and they do not have a rest mass. Thus, the concept of a material object does not apply to photons. In a similar vein, does the concept 'person' apply to God?

Normally, we simply assume that we can use the following pairs of words to characterize God: 'being' and 'non-being' and 'person' and 'non person.' However, this assumption seems problematic. We know the difference between beings and non-beings from our everyday experience. We know that stones and flowers are not beings, and that rabbits and birds are. We learn how to apply this distinction to things in the garden of experience. The distinction has a function in relation to experience. Similar points apply to the contrast between person and non-person. However, when these distinctions are used in relation to God, the terms 'being' and 'non being' (and 'person' and 'non-person') are used beyond experience. In what sense is God a being? He is not like a rabbit or even a human. Does this imply that He is not a being? This would mean He is like a stone. Or rather is it that these terms do not apply to God, just as the terms 'hot' and 'cold' do not?

Is God a person? This requires us to answer the question, 'What is a person?' Prima facie, it is reasonable to characterize a person partly in biological terms, since a person must be alive, and being alive should be specified in terms of biological functions, such as reproduction. These functions obviously do not apply to God.

Perhaps, that was too quick and easy. Alternatively, we could characterize a person as an entity that can have self-conscious mental states. This is a commonly accepted definition and appears less prejudicial against God being a person because it does not wear a biological requirement on its sleeve.

Now, it is a defining feature of mental states that they are intentional (see page 74). They must be about something. To think is to think that P. Similar points apply to believing, wanting and willing. In each case, what follows the 'that' clause specifies the content of the mental state.

However, for a mental state to be about something, it must be not about other things. To think one thing is to not think another. Furthermore, the content of mental states, such as beliefs, thoughts, desires and fears, is partly dependent on how they are described. The truth of sentences formed from such psychological verbs depends on how the thing in question is described, i.e. from what angle or aspect it is described. For example, John wants a new job under one description, but not under another (see pages 62 and 80). In this way, the intentionality of mental states is an expression of our finitude. This is because, whenever we believe and desire, it is necessarily partial, reflecting a particular point of view to the exclusion of others.

Can God have mental states? The answer to this question must be no, if intentionality is a necessary feature of mental states. If God is not finite, then for Him to think one thing must be for Him to think everything, from all points of view, under all possible descriptions, all at once. Otherwise, God's thoughts would reflect partiality or finitude, which is impossible. (To claim that God can be both finite and infinite, only makes the problem worse, because it implies that God can have contradictory properties). Consequently, whatever God does should not be called intentional thought. In other words, whatever we are tempted to call 'God's thoughts' cannot be thoughts at all. Worse still, doing and action implies desire and belief. Actions are caused by desires and beliefs. Consequently, 'does,' and other action words, cannot be predicated of God, if God cannot be said to think and want. In brief, God does not have mental states.

If He cannot have mental states, then this implies that He is not a person, given the definition of 'person' with which we began: anything that can have self-conscious mental states. However, we should not conclude from this that God is a non-person, because that would imply that He is an inert thing like a stone. It would be more accurate to say that God is beyond the person/non-person dichotomy. It would be better to claim that God is trans-personal. In reply to these points, a traditional theist might claim that, when we affirm that God wants or thinks, we are not employing these words in their ordinary sense. However, that is exactly my point.

Conclusion

If God is an entity or being which is in, or is part of, the universe, then either He exists or He does not. If God is not a possible entity in the universe, then, given that the concept of God makes sense, there are only two possibilities left:

1. God transcends the universe and this would imply that God transcends the pair of terms 'exists' and 'does not exist.'
2. God is the universe, or some aspect of it. In which case, the existence of God would depend on whether the universe as a whole has the required characteristics or not.

In either of these two cases, even given that the concept of the divine makes sense, the traditional definition of God is mistaken.

40

4

Making the World Vanish

We are going to play a game, which consists in betting which of two sides in a debate will win. Although the debate is academic, who wins has some importance for our view of the world. How will you bet? Best to calculate the odds by examining the arguments.

Step 1: Setting Things Up

First, let us set up the problem. What is to know something? Why is this question important? Philosophical thinking about the nature of knowledge rose to prominence in the seventeenth century, at the dawn of the modern period. Prior to that, in the medieval period, people tended to accept things on the basis of authority alone. During the modern period, thinkers such as Galileo, Bacon and Descartes first developed the scientific method. They replaced appeals to authority with observation and reasoning. Up to the late 16th century, a common form of scholarly argument for a thesis was to amass relevant supportive quotations and references from authoritative sources, such as Aristotle and the *Bible*. However, astronomy and mathematics required a different type of demonstration, and their development was, therefore, important to the process of replacing arguments from authority with observation and reasoning.

41

Because of these developments, during the modern period, there was a collision of two world-views. It became clear that the scientific method leads to a picture of the universe quite opposed to that of the traditional religious views of the earlier medieval period. Science portrays the universe as a physical and mechanical system, which apparently has no place for consciousness, God, and even moral values. Because of this conflict of world-views, it became important to discover the foundations of knowledge. How else could the conflict be resolved, except by self-conscious reflection upon the sources and standards of knowledge? It became important to ask, 'What should count as knowledge, and on what basis?' and 'How should we justify claims to know?' Thinkers could re-evaluate the nature of humanity's place in the universe only by answering such questions. Today, these conflicts have not been completely resolved. There is still an extraordinary tension between what we think we know about the world, and what science tells us about it. There will be more about this in Chapter 8.

What is knowledge? Typically, a definition consists of a set of conditions that are both necessary and sufficient. For instance, to be a brother, it is necessary to be a male. It is also necessary to be a sibling. To be a brother, it is sufficient to be both, i.e. a male sibling. This gives us a definition of 'brother' in terms of necessary and sufficient conditions. However, many concepts are not as clear-cut as that. Often, it is not easy, or even possible, to define a word in terms of necessary and sufficient conditions.

One cannot define knowing in terms of having information. Suppose your company needs to know the sales records of its competitor. Secretly, you enter the competitor's office to grab their records. Back in your own office, when your boss asks you whether you have the information, he is asking for the computer discs in your hand, not whether you know what those disks contain. Knowledge is not merely having information.

The standard view claims that there are three necessary conditions for knowledge, which are together sufficient. These are that, in order to know something,

1. One must believe it
2. What one believes is true.
3. One has reasonable justification for one's belief.

There are problems with the standard view, but these need not concern us here. If the third condition is correct, then having reasonable evidence is a necessary condition of knowledge. In other words, in order to have knowledge, you must have evidence. This means that you could believe something that is true and still not know it. For example, you believe that the horse Sandy Ears will win the three o'clock race. She wins. However, your lucky guess would not count as knowledge, because you had no justification or evidence for the belief. Please note that I used the expression 'reasonable evidence' rather than the word 'proof.' 'Proof' implies a very strong requirement. One can know many things that one cannot prove, because one can have reasonable evidence, which is something less than conclusive proof.

Step 2: Planting the Seeds of Doubt

We think that we know that the world consists of the objects in space and time that we perceive daily. But do we really know this? Against commonsense, some philosophers have insisted that it is impossible to be sure.

Others have argued that we can be certain that matter is an illusion and that the world does not consist of material things at all. The Hindu and Buddhists traditions claim that the world as we experience it is an illusion and that this fact has great moral importance for the spiritual development of the individual. The spiritual quest of any being is to overcome and be free of the illusion. When one finally pierces the veil of illusion and achieves Nirvana, one will realize that everyday experience is like a dream. One will experience the universe as it really is: an indivisible whole. In contrast, in everyday experience, we create divisions in the wholeness of the One, and this is an illusion.

These claims are not mere speculations. They are based on apparently strong arguments, which we are going to examine. For instance, the Irish philosopher Berkeley (1685-1703) argued that we can be certain that material objects do not exist at all. His arguments are difficult to resist.

Are you ready to place your first bet? Will you deny or affirm that the world we perceive is, in some sense, an illusion? Be careful. When we deny that the objects we see are illusions, we are claiming that these mystical and religious views of the world are mistaken. To do that, we had better have some evidence or argument. Merely appealing to commonsense is not an argument. If such views are wrong, why are they?

Let me plant the seeds of doubt. Let us return to the idea that we cannot be sure that the world is as it appears. In his *Meditations,* the French philosopher Descartes (1596-1650) doubts that we can have knowledge of the external world. He tries to show that such doubt is reasonable, so that later he can rebuild knowledge on a certain foundation. In the first Meditation, he argues that we cannot have knowledge of the external world. This is an extraordinary conclusion to reach. It implies that you do not know that you are wearing shoes.

To show that such doubts are well founded, Descartes claims that there could be a very powerful, deceiving demon, causing him to have the ideas of a material world. He could be deceived even concerning the belief that external objects exist. (This is sometimes called the third stage of doubt). Descartes is not making the extravagant claim that there really is a deceiving demon; he is only asserting that there could be one. In other words, he is affirming that he has no evidence to show that there is not one. The ideas or sensations we experience could be equally well caused by material objects or by a powerful deceiving spirit. In other words, we have no evidence to show that theory A) is more likely to be true than theory B):

A) The sensations I am now having are caused by material objects.

B) The sensations I am having are caused by a deceiving demon

In science there is a phenomenon called the underdetermination of theory by data. This occurs when there are at least two conflicting hypotheses that equally well explain a set of given data. In other words, the data are insufficient to decide which of the two hypotheses is true and which is false. This is underdetermination of theory by data.

According to Descartes, the situation with respect to perception is similar. In contemporary scientific language, the data are insufficient to determine the theory. In this case, the data are our ideas or sensations, and the competing theories are A and B above. We have no evidence to think that hypothesis A is true and that hypothesis B is false and, consequently, it is reasonable to doubt the existence of material objects.

This does not mean that there are no material objects, but only that we cannot truly claim to know that there are material objects. Such a knowledge claim requires reasonable justification, which we lack. Furthermore, Descartes' conclusion does not leave it open for individuals to decide for themselves whether external objects exist. His claim is not that, in the absence of evidence, you can choose whichever theory you want. Accepting or choosing a hypothesis means thinking that it is true and, without any evidence, there is no reason for picking one as true and not the other. Descartes' argument is as follows:

1. There could be a powerful demon deceiving me
2. If there were a demon, then I would be mistaken in my beliefs
3. Therefore, my beliefs could be mistaken

Has Descartes made a mistake? Is there evidence that you are not being deceived by a demon? If there is, then premise one is false.

However, the fact that one does like Descartes' conclusion does not count as evidence. Neither does the vague thought that there must be something wrong with his reasoning. Imagine Descartes is sitting here with us. Let us dust him down a bit. You say to Descartes: 'You are mistaken. There must be something wrong with your argument, because I know that I know many things about the external world.' How would he respond? Probably as follows: 'You claim to know. But knowledge requires reasonable evidence. What support do you have for the claim that you know? I have given you an argument that you do not know.' How will you answer Descartes?

Now is your second opportunity to bet. Considering the argument, do you think that Descartes is right? If you do not, what is your reply to him? And how would he reply in turn to you? If knowledge requires reasonable justification, which we do not have, then we do not know. I insist that you address this problem and feel its force, without trying to escape it by loose thinking, which will not help you become a better thinker. Now that my short sermon is over, please bet.

In fact, there is a weakness in Descartes argument. It assumes that a person can be directly acquainted only with his or her own ideas or sensations. By describing ideas as the basic data, the argument assumes that we only perceive our own ideas and sensations. From this assumption, it follows that the existence of material objects is an underdetermined hypothesis. However, as we shall now see, this assumption has a very forceful argument to back it up.

Step 3: Making the World Vanish

Are bananas really yellow? To answer this apparently absurd question, we shall make two boxes. One is titled 'ideas in the mind,' and the other 'the real properties of things in the world.' Clearly the feeling of pain when one holds a hot poker is an idea in the mind, which belongs in the first box. Your pain is not a property of the poker itself, although the poker causes it. In that case, the physical cause of the pain belongs in the second box, 'properties in the real world.'

You are frying onions and there is a smell. Is the smell an idea in your mind, or is it a property out there in the real world? Which box does the smell go into? The smell has a physical cause or basis, which is the structure of the molecules wafting through the air. However, is the smell itself the same as that molecular structure? One argument concludes that they are not identical because that same smell could be caused by other chemical structures. For instance, if I hypnotized you appropriately and placed a bottle of ammonia under your nose, you would have the smell of fried onions. It seems that we should conclude that the real smell is the sensation you perceive, and that is an idea in the mind, which goes in box 1. Consequently, it seems that the molecular structure is the cause of that smell (rather than the smell itself), and goes in box 2, under the list of real properties in the world.

Is the banana really yellow? Again, colors have a physical basis, which is the wavelength of the reflected light. However, once again that cannot be identical to the color seen, because you can perceive an object reflecting light of another wavelength as yellow, for instance, if you have jaundice or are wearing yellow glasses. That vibrant yellow you perceive, therefore, should go into box 1 - ideas in the mind.

This type of argument also applies to the sounds we hear, and the tastes we experience and it forms the basis of the argument from illusion.

1. The real properties of an external object cannot change without a change occurring in the object itself.
2. The colors I perceive can change without the occurrence of a change in the object itself.
3. Therefore, the colors I perceive are not the real properties of an external object.

Once this conclusion is reached, it is apparently but a short step to the conclusion that the colors I see must be ideas in my mind. The same form of argument can be repeated for other sensory qualities, such as the sounds we hear, the odors we smell, and so on. The above argument needs an explanation.

a) Premise 1: The real properties of an external object cannot change without there being some change in the object itself.

This first premise gives a test or a criterion for what is to count as the real properties of an external object. It claims that anything that is a property of this kind has to be such that, if it changes, then there has to be an alteration in the object. For example, your height is a property or a characteristic of you, which cannot vary without there being a change in you. By definition, the real properties of an external object cannot alter without there being some modification in the object itself.

b) Premise 2: The smell I perceive can change without there being any change in the object itself.

46

For example, if I am drunk, the smell changes, even though the object remains the same. If I am hypnotized, the smell I perceive will change even though there will be no physical alteration in the object. Therefore, the smell can change without the object altering. In other words, the smell I perceive has failed the test that the properties of a real object have to satisfy.

c) These two premises imply the conclusion 3 that the smell I perceive is not the property of a real object.

Let us examine the final step by adding another premise:

Premise 4: Either the smell you perceive is a real property of an external object or it's an idea in the mind.

Given premise 4, and the conclusion 3, we must conclude that

5. The smell I perceive is an idea in my mind.

It seems clear that the taste of pineapples, the color of bananas and the smell of fried onions are ideas in the mind. Now, one could claim that the real taste and the real smell result from the molecular structure of the object. However, if the argument from illusion is sound, then it follows logically that the smell you perceive, and so on, cannot be any of these properties of external objects, but are ideas in the mind. These are experiences that belong in box 1 and not box 2.

Primary and Secondary Qualities

Clearly, the argument from illusion applies to the colors, tastes, smells, and sounds we perceive. For this reason, the empiricist John Locke (1632-1704) placed them in box 2 and called them the ideas of secondary qualities (for a qualification, see Thomson, 2001a). However, he also claimed that there are primary qualities that belong to the object itself. These include size, shape, mass, and duration. According to him, these spatio-temporal properties of an object belong to the object itself. They belong in box 2, properties in the real world.

Locke thought that philosophical reflection on the science of the 17th century shows us that colors do not belong to the object at all. In a way, our senses trick us. We think that the colors we see are out there in the world, when they are not. The point also applies to the sounds we hear, which are only ideas in the mind.

What about when an ice cube melts because of the heat? Surely, the heat is out there in the external world. Locke's point is that hot and cold as I perceive them can change without any alteration in the object. For example, after being outside in the winter, the room you enter will feel hot. In the summer, a room at the same temperature feels cool. Consequently, because the argument from illusion applies to the heat we perceive, it is not the real property of the object and belongs in box 1 (ideas in the mind). However, Locke added that the vibration of molecules, composed of primary qualities, is part of the object and belongs in box 2.

Berkeley opposed Locke's distinction between primary and secondary qualities, claiming that the argument from illusion applies to the primary qualities as well. For instance, the shapes and sizes you see can change without there being any modification in the object. A distant tower looks small but, from close up, it appears large. From an angle, a circle looks like an oval. Thus, the shapes and sizes we perceive are not real properties of external objects. Berkeley also claims that the argument from illusion also applies to the weights we feel, to the perception of duration, and to all the primary qualities, which must be ideas in the mind.

Berkeley's argument presents us with a difficult choice. He claims that every single sensible quality that we perceive can change without there being any modification in the object. This means we have to choose: either

a) Sensible qualities are perceivable, in which case they are merely ideas, or else,
b) If they are real properties in the external world, then they are not perceivable.

In other words, if size is something one knows and sees, then it cannot be part of an object. On the other hand, if size is a real property of an external object, then one has to admit that one cannot see it. In which case, it becomes impossible to sustain that you can know it, Consequently, the real properties of objects are all unknowns. Everything we know and perceive should go into box 1, and what remains for box 2 is something essentially unknown.

By applying the argument from illusion to both perceived secondary and primary qualities, Berkeley concludes that

6. We can only perceive our own ideas.

This is a remarkable conclusion. It means, for example, that the claim that you can perceive your hands is mistaken.

Locke argues that our ideas of primary qualities resemble the qualities themselves in the world. In reply, Berkeley notes that one cannot step outside of one's ideas to compare them directly to the world. Such a comparison requires direct perception of the world, which is impossible. Since to perceive is to have ideas, the only access we have to the world is indirect, through our ideas. There is no possibility of comparing ideas and external objects, because we can only perceive our own ideas.

If Berkeley is right, we do not even perceive our own bodies. Instead, we have ideas that are caused by something out there, which we call our body. Consequently, the scientific causal explanation of perception is misleading. For visual perception, the normal account claims that the light reflected by an object strikes the retina and stimulates the optical nerve, which stimulates the brain, causing an idea in the mind. If Berkeley is right, then this explanation is misleading because we do not have direct knowledge of eyes, retinal nerves, and brains. Direct knowledge is restricted to our own ideas.

According to this view, how do we form the concept of external things? Our ideas have coherence and an order, due to which, we form the concept of external objects. Forming this concept is not a simple task. It takes children several months, even though they are young and most capable of learning. Due to this order in our ideas, we interpret experience as being of objects that can exist unperceived. But this does not mean that we really perceive such objects. We only see colors and shapes, which we interpret in this way. The order and coherence among those ideas is what allows us to live practically, but it does not give us knowledge of the external world.

This leads to another point in favor of Berkeley. There is a difference between the raw experience itself and the experience as it is usually interpreted. Thought and sensation are distinct. For example, looking down the street, you think that you see a friend. The shape you see looks familiar, but as you get closer, you realize that it is just a shadow. Your interpretation affected your perception. When we experience sensations without adding in any interpretation, we perceive the experience as it is without thought. Try to describe your experience without adding in any interpretation. As you concentrate on the nature of the sensation itself, the interpretation becomes less strong, until you perceive raw sensations, without adding the interpretation that they are of external objects. It seems that we impose the concept of material objects on our experience of ideas. Normally, we assume that our vision is taking us out there, to the object itself. Berkeley's arguments attempt to show us that this assumption is a false interpretation.

Conclusions

Have you made your bet? If you opted in favor of Descartes or Berkeley, then you have a problem. How do we bridge the gap between our personal experience of ideas and our claims to know the external world? How is our claim to know so much about the world justifiable, if we do not even perceive objects? This chapter has been in part an extended example of the first stage of philosophy: questioning and being puzzled. The arguments apparently show that we do not perceive external objects, but only ideas. This lands us with the problem: How is it possible to have knowledge of material objects? It seems that it must be impossible. We can know patterns among our sensations, but never the external world itself. If all knowledge is based on sense-experience, then the nature of the world must be forever a mystery.

5

Against Private Objects

The argument from illusion appears to be sound, despite the dramatic and counter-intuitive nature of its implications. It entails that we can only perceive our own ideas, and that we cannot ever directly perceive external objects. It implies that we are forever locked in the prison of our own consciousness, without direct access to the external world. This position is inherent in the philosophies of Descartes (1596-1650), and the empiricists, Locke (1632-1704), Berkeley (1685-1753), and Hume (1711-1776). The alternative position would be to affirm that we can directly perceive material objects. However, this position so far has only commonsense to recommend it and, moreover, the argument from illusion apparently shows it to be mistaken. Once again, it is time to place your bets, as now we shall examine this alternative position.

The Hallucination

Imagine a person who claims to see a castle in the complete darkness of a sensory-deprivation tank. Alternatively, imagine a person in an empty desert, who sees the mirage of an oasis. Such persons might reason as follows:

7. I am seeing something
8. I am not seeing an external object
9. Given that I am seeing something then, either I am seeing an external object or I am seeing my own ideas
10. Therefore, I am seeing my own ideas.

The above argument has a fatal flaw: premise 7 begs the question. The premise assumes that there must be some *thing* that the person is seeing when he or she undergoes a hallucination. It is only given this assumption that we can draw the conclusion that the thing being seen cannot be a material object and, therefore, must be some mental idea.

Obviously, a person having a hallucination is seeing, and his or her experience has a content. But we should not assume that this implies that he or she must be seeing some *thing*. We cannot assume that the experiential content of a person's seeing is the object of experience, or is the thing seen. To make that assumption is to assume that ideas exist as mental entities.

The alternative to this assumption would be to argue that a person who is hallucinating is not seeing any *thing*. This alternative would admit that such a person is seeing, but would deny that this content is the *object* of his or her experience. In other words, the alternative would be to reject the claim implicit in premise 7 that the content of experience is a mental object. We could argue that the experiential content of the seeing is simply a way of seeing, and we could treat experience adverbially rather than as an object (I will explain this later).

To avoid begging the question, we should replace premise 7 with

7*. I am having a visual experience.

However, if we replace premise 7 in the original argument with 7*, the argument becomes invalid. The conclusion does not follow from the new set of premises. Without some independent support for the claim that premise 7 is true and that statement 7* is false, the argument from hallucination begs the question.

A Criticism of the Argument from Illusion

This criticism of the argument from hallucination can be used to criticize the argument from illusion, since the two arguments are similar. This point is important because the argument from illusion is the main support for the positions advocated by Descartes and Berkeley. In Chapter 4, premise 2 of the argument from illusion was:

2. The colors I perceive can change without the occurrence of a change in the object itself.

This premise, like premise 7, begs the question. Premise 2 assumes that the colors I perceive are mental objects or ideas. It assumes that what can change (without there being any alteration in the external object) is some *thing,* which I perceive. Against this second premise, we could argue that what can change (without any alteration in the external object) is not some *thing,* but is the way we perceive, or the phenomenological content of our perceiving. For instance, the way in which I perceive a white wall will alter when the color of the light changes. Against this second premise, we could also insist that what I perceive is the color of an external object, and that this objective color cannot change without any alteration in the object itself. To be more precise, we could replace premise 2 with

2*. The way I perceive color can change without any alteration in the object itself.

Once we replace 2 with 2*, the argument is no longer valid. Without some new independent support for the claim that premise 2 is true and statement 2* is false, the argument from illusion begs the question. It no longer provides evidence for the conclusion that
6) We can only perceive our own ideas.

An Alternative View: Direct Realism

At most, we may conclude that the argument from illusion does not establish the conclusion that we can only perceive our own ideas. Of course, this does not imply that the conclusion itself is false. The argument from illusion is inconclusive, but the conclusion (namely, that we only perceive our own ideas) could still be true.

For the moment, instead of arguing that the conclusion is false, let us see what an alternative view would be like. The alternative position, called direct realism, holds that we can directly perceive external objects, and that the objects of perception are not ideas in the mind. Developing direct realism is important, because the claim that we can only perceive our own ideas is a central pillar in the philosophies of Descartes, and the empiricists. Kant, on the other hand, is a direct realist, because he claims that we perceive directly objects in space and time.

Phrases, such as 'I see something' and 'what I see,' are ambiguous. They could refer to the content of the seeing (i.e. the experiential nature of the visual experience itself). Alternatively, such phrases could refer to the thing seen, an external object which exists independently of the act of seeing. According to the direct realist, we should clearly distinguish the content of seeing from the thing seen. The experiential content of my seeing is not an object over and above the act of seeing; it is merely the way or manner in which I see. The independent object of my perception, the thing I actually see, such as a tree, is something quite distinct from my act of seeing. It exists whether I look at it or not.

According to the direct realist, when we suffer from a hallucination, we do not see any thing. While we assert that such a person is seeing something, this simply means that he or she is seeing in a particular manner. The direct realist asserts that it is tempting, but misleading, to claim that there is a mental thing that such a person perceives. It is misleading because it implies that there is some *thing*, some actual mental object, which the person perceives.

The English language is not conducive to the making of a clear distinction between the content of seeing and the object seen. For example, the question 'What are you seeing?' could be a request either to describe the experience as such to describe the external object which is being seen.

According to the direct realist, the failure to distinguish the content of experience from the independent object experienced causes confusion. It can lead us to reify the experiential content of the experience or, in other words, to treat it as if it were the object perceived. Descartes, Locke, and Berkeley use the word 'idea' to refer to the content of experiences, but they treat this content as if it were a mental item or a picture in the mind. In contrast, the direct realist claims that ideas are *not* objects over and above the act of seeing itself. Ideas are not the objects of perception; they are the way or manner in which we see. The direct realist argues that Locke, Descartes and Berkeley are mistaken to claim that we perceive our own ideas. Ideas are not the objects we see, because they are not objects at all.

To make the point clear, we might compare ideas to moods (Bennett, 1979 and Jenkins, 1983, p.77-81). The direct realist claims that moods are not mental items. Although, in English, we do refer to moods as *what* we feel, the direct realist would not think of a mood as an object. A mood is nothing over and above feeling a certain way. Rather than asking a person '*What* do you feel?' as if the person were feeling a thing, it would be more accurate to ask '*How* do you feel?' Just as moods are the way we feel, ideas are simply the manner in which we perceive. Consequently, we should not be misled by the

English language into treating the content of perception as an object. Ideas are not what we perceive; they are the way we perceive.

Of course, none of the above constitutes an argument for direct realism. Nor does it constitute an argument against the claim that we can only perceive our own ideas. It merely indicates how one might develop an alternative view.

The Private Language Argument

There might be an argument against the claim that we can only perceive our own ideas. The Austrian philosopher Wittgenstein (1889-1951) advanced the private language argument, which seems to challenge the heart of Descartes' and Berkeley's claim that the immediate objects of perception are ideas in the mind.

In his first Meditation, Descartes doubts the existence of the external world. He has ideas, which he can identify directly, but he does not know whether anything 'out there' in the external world really corresponds or causes those ideas. Descartes is imprisoned in the world of his own immediate ideas. We can call this, Descartes' original position. According to Descartes, the only way out of this prison is to prove the existence of God, and thereby vindicate the principle that clear and distinct ideas are true. This principle serves as a knowledge-bridge from ideas to the world. However, if we cannot prove the existence of God, this way-out is not open to us.

Is Descartes' original position viable? Wittgenstein's argument claims to show that it is not. Descartes assumes that, when he thinks 'perhaps an evil demon exists,' the words employed to express such thoughts do have meaning. In his method of doubt, the meaning of words are treated as a given, and not subjected to the process of doubt to which Descartes is otherwise committed. Is Descartes entitled to this given, meaningful language? Wittgenstein offers an argument to show that he is not because words are, and must be, common currency in the public domain. Linguistic meaning requires the existence of an objective world, and cannot be exclusive to Descartes' private ideas.

In brief, Wittgenstein argues against the possibility of an essentially private language. He imagines a person who uses the letter 'S' to refer to a sensation. When the sensation occurs again, the person intends to use 'S' to refer to the same sensation. Now, in the normal course of life, we often identify sensations by their cause (e.g. the feeling when I hear chalk being scraped on the board). However, such ways of identifying sensations presuppose the existence of the external world, and that is prohibited to anyone in Descartes' original position. Descartes' method of doubt requires an essentially private language,

55

Against Private Objects

one that obtains its meaning directly by referring to the privately felt quality of sensations, or to their introspective feel, without relying on external causal factors. Wittgenstein's argument against the possibility of an essentially private language (an EPL) is:

1. Meaningful word usage requires the possibility of error
2. In an EPL, there is no possibility of a distinction between X appears to be right and X is right
3. Therefore a meaningful EPL is impossible

The first premise claims that meaning requires that the mistaken employment of a word is possible, such as calling a dog 'a cat.' The second states that in an essentially private language, there is no possibility of such misapplication of words because, in the private realm, there is no possible distinction between how things are and how they seem. If I have a sensation which seems to me to be S, then in the essentially private realm, nothing possibly can count as my being mistaken. Wittgenstein says 'Whatever is going to seem right to me is right and that only means that here we cannot talk of 'right'' (Wittgenstein, 1953, paragraph 258).

Please note that the second premise does *not* assert that we cannot verify whether we have made a mistake in the identification of our own sensations, but rather that, in the private realm, there is no possibility of error. It is not a question of possibility of verification, but of the possibility of error.

Descartes' method of doubt is first–person singular. Instead of asking 'What can *we* know?' he asks 'What can *I* know?' Thus, Descartes finds himself in the cage of his own ideas, wondering whether anything in the external world that matches them. Had Descartes asked the first question, he would not be in this 'egocentric predicament' (Williams, 1978). If he had asked 'What can *we* know?' then, he would have already committed himself to the existence of other minds, and to a common public world in which they live. The private language argument shows that we are committed to such a world, because language is meaningful. Descartes' original position is mistaken. We are part of the misnamed external world.

Another Implication

Descartes and the empiricists reified ideas. This led to the notion of a veil of ideas, beyond which we can never directly perceive. The private language argument rejects this veil, by arguing that sensation words, such as 'pain,' cannot name essentially private mental objects.

This lets of us off the hook concerning the problems of perception presented in the previous chapter. We can affirm that Berkeley and Descartes are mistaken to affirm that we can only perceive our own ideas. In this way we can avoid their skeptical conclusions about perception. We can affirm that we do perceive shoes and hands. However, the denial of private ideas has very dramatic consequences for the mind-body problem and the nature of consciousness.

We like to think of experience as revealing an inner subjective world, which is described in poetry, and which should be contrasted with the external world. But, if there are no private mental objects, then there is no such inner world. Or, at least, it is wrong to call it 'a world.' The denial of private mental objects means that there is no such *thing* as experience. Perhaps, this is a drastic way to put the point. It does not deny the fact that people perceive. It rejects that perceptions are things, but it does not deny that people experience; rather it denies that experience is a *thing*.

Regarding ideas as mental objects leads to mind/body dualism, the proposition that the mind is a non-material entity. If ideas are private mental objects, then it is reasonable to treat the mind as a non-physical container, which possesses or holds those non-physical ideas. On the other hand, if there are no private mental objects or ideas, then we should not conceive of the mind as a thing at all, and dualism is mistaken. This means that to defend mind/body dualism and the idea that experience reveals an inner subjective world, you have to affirm that the private language argument is unsound, and assert that ideas are private mental objects after all. However, this would be bad news. It would mean that we are saddled once again with the skeptical view of perception outlined in the previous chapter. It would mean that Descartes and Berkeley were right after all.

In conclusion, the problem of perception is deeply linked to the mind/body question. In the case of perception, the problem is how to proceed from 'in here' to what is 'out there.' In the case of the mind/body, the problem is how to pass from what is 'out here' to what is 'in there.' Both problems require the internal/external or the inner/outer contrast, which Wittgenstein's private language argument rejects. It denies that this as a contrast between two worlds. It repudiates the internal/external as an ontological distinction, because it renounces the claim that ideas are things. If the contrast is mistaken in the case of perception, then it must be too in the case of the mind/body problem.

6

Mind and Brain

I am only this physical body? On the one hand, it seems that I must be more than just that, because how could I be conscious, if I were no more than a collection of cells? How can a collection of cells have a subjective point of view on the universe? Yet, on the other hand, the natural sciences tell us that the universe consists of no more than matter and its physical properties. Commonsense and science conflict. Which is right? It appears that either the conscious mind challenges the scientific picture of the universe, or that the scientific picture throws into doubt our normal understanding of ourselves.

The conflict first arose during the modern period, approximately 1550-1750, because of fundamental changes in our view of matter. Before the modern period, the universe was considered to be like a living being or organism. Physical changes were explained according to purposes: nature *hates* a vacuum; storms occur because God is *angry*. During the modern period, this view was rejected and replaced by the conception of matter as something inert that changes according to mathematically definable laws. This mechanical view of matter made mathematically based science and measurement possible.

The new view of matter threw into sharp relief the contrast between the physical universe and the human mind, which is animate, conscious, rational and free. How is it possible to reconcile the scientific view of the physical universe, with our view of ourselves as part of that universe, but essentially non-mechanistic and conscious?

Today, we who have benefited so much from the technology developed from this view of science are still in the grips of this same conflict and crisis. In this chapter and the next two, we shall look at three levels of answer to these questions. Some writers confuse these three levels, and I shall show how we may attain much greater clarity, and even answers, by separating them. Furthermore, this clarity will help us gain insight into the nature of science.

THE FIRST LEVEL: THE ONTOLOGICAL

As one of the pioneers of the new science, Descartes tried to apply the principles of mechanistic explanation to a wide range of natural phenomena, such as planetary motion, light, the tides, and to the functions of the human body, such as the circulation of the blood and respiration. He claimed that the mechanical motion of matter could explain all physical phenomena.

Dualism

However, according to Descartes, scientific explanation should stop there. He thought that the actions and mental states of persons could not be so explained. Descartes argued that a person is an essentially conscious and non-material substance or thing. Accordingly, the universe contains at least two kinds of substances: mind, whose essence is to be conscious, and matter, whose essence is spatial. What is a human being? According to Descartes, we are these two distinct substances in intimate causal relations. Changes in the mind constantly cause changes in the body and vice versa. Descartes has two arguments to support his contention that the mind and body are distinct.

A. The Argument from Doubt

In the *Discourse on the Method*, Descartes argues as follows:

Argument 1

1. I cannot doubt that I (as a mind) exist.
2. I can doubt that my body exists.
3. Therefore, I (as a mind) am distinct from my body.

Descartes thinks that he can doubt that his body exists because the existence of any material object behind the veil of perception can be doubted (see Chapter 4 below). In contrast, he claims that he cannot doubt the existence of his mind, because he is immediately aware of the fact that he is conscious, even in the very act of doubting.

59

Argument 1 relies on the principle of the indiscernibility of identicals. This principle states that identicals, such as water and H_2O, must have all properties in common. If water had a property that was not shared by H_2O, then the two could not be identical. In more technical terms, if X is the same object or identical with Y then any predicate, F, true of X must also be true of Y.

Descartes relies on this principle when he argues as follows. If my mind were identical to my body, then what is true of the one must also be true of the other; but there is one thing that is true of my mind that is not true of my body, namely that I cannot doubt that it exists. We can reformulate the argument from doubt more accurately as follows:

Argument 2

1. If two things are identical, then they must have all of their properties in common.
2. My mind has the property that I cannot doubt that it exists.
3. My body does not have this property.
4. Therefore, my mind and my body are not identical

Descartes' argument is not valid, and this can be seen from an example. Water and H_2O are identical, but the above argument could be applied to them. A person who is ignorant of chemistry, who does not what H_2O is, could argue as follows:

Argument 3

1. If water and H_2O were identical, then they must have all their properties in common.
2. Water has the property that I do not doubt that it exists.
3. H_2O does not have this property, because I do doubt that it exists.
4. Therefore, water and H_2O cannot be identical.

Since we know that water and H_2O are identical, there must be something wrong with this argument; it must be unsound. However, Descartes' argument from doubt (argument 2 above) has the same basic logical form as this unsound argument, and so it too must be unsound.

The two arguments are not sound, because they involve psychological phenomena, such as doubting, believing and wanting, which form non–extensional contexts (see page 79). A context is simply a part of sentence: for example, 'is red,' 'John believes that....' are contexts, which when they are combined with suitable phrases make a complete sentence. Many inferences that are valid for extensional contexts are invalid for non–extensional or intensional contexts.

In an extensional context, when we substitute for a word any other term that refers to the same thing, then this will not change the truth or falsity of the whole sentence. The substitution of the word 'Gorbachov' by the phrase 'the ex-President of the USSR' will not change the truth-value of the sentence 'Gorbachov is bald.' Consequently, the context 'is bald' is extensional. Because of this, the following argument is logically valid:

Argument 4

1. Gorbachov is bald.
2. The ex-President of the USSR is the same person as Gorbachov.
3. Therefore, the ex-President of the USSR is bald.

On the other hand, in an intensional context, when we substitute a word with any other term that refers to the same thing, then this may change the truth of the whole sentence. For example, 'Dan believes that Gorbachov is bald' is true. But, even though Gorbachov and the ex-President of the USSR are the same person, the sentence 'Dan believes that the ex-President of USSR is bald' may not be true (for example, if Dan believes that Gorbachov was the president of Roumania). The substitution of the word 'Gorbachov' by 'the ex-President of the USSR' may change the truth of the whole sentence; consequently the context 'Dan believes that' is intensional. Because of this, the following argument is not logically valid:

Argument 5

1. Dan believes that Gorbachov is bald.
2. Michael is the same person as ex-President of the USSR.
3. Therefore, Dan believes that ex-President of the USSR is bald.

For similar reasons, the following argument, which is similar to Descartes' argument 2 and to argument 3, is also invalid:

Argument 6

1. Dan believes that Gorbachov is bald.
2. Dan does not believe that the USSR President is bald.
3. Therefore, Gorbachov is not the President of the USSR.

61

Like 'believes,' 'doubts' is intensional and so Descartes' argument from doubt is invalid and fails to prove that the mind and the body are distinct. We cannot infer from subjective doubt about X and lack of doubt about Y to conclude that X and Y are objectively non–identical.

B. The Argument from Divisibility

In his second argument for mind/body dualism, Descartes contends that he is an indivisible thing. But matter, being extended, is always divisible. Hence, Descartes concludes that he must be different in kind from all matter, including his own body.

Argument 7

1. The mind is an indivisible thing.
2. All material objects must be spatially extended.
3. <u>Anything that is spatially extended is divisible</u>.
4. Therefore, the mind is not a material object.

There are three problems with this argument. First, in what sense is the mind indivisible? Sibyl was a famous example of a person with several split personalities. Some people have had the connection between the two hemispheres of the their brain severed. In such cases, the left-hand side of the brain does not know what the right hand side of the brain is seeing, when it is deprived of the visual information under certain experimental conditions. Do these count as indivisible minds? Perhaps, the mind is not indivisible after all.

Furthermore, in a valid argument, words in the premises must be used with the same sense. The word 'bat' has two meanings and, consequently, the following is not a valid argument:

Argument 8

1. He hit the ball with a bat.
2. <u>A bat is an animal</u>.
3. Therefore, he hit the ball with an animal.

It is not valid because the word 'bat' has a different meaning in the two premises. Argument 7 suffers from the same problem. The sense in which the mind is indivisible is different from the meaning of 'divisible' when applied to material objects. Objects are divisible because they can be cut up into pieces. Minds are not the kinds of things that can or cannot be cut up into pieces. The way in which the mind is allegedly indivisible is quite different from the manner in which, say, a photon is indivisible. Thus, Descartes' argument 7 trades on an ambiguity.

The third problem concerns premise one. Descartes just assumes that the mind is an object. We shall examine reasons for rejecting this premise below. For instance, the mind would have to be a non-spatial object and it is not clear that such a notion makes sense.

Problems with Dualism

We will briefly examine four major objections to dualism.

1. The Causal Connection

Descartes holds that there is a two–way causal interaction between the mind and the body. In sense perception, neural impulses in the brain affect the mind. For instance, in seeing an object, light waves reflected by that object affect the eye and the brain, and the changes in the brain cause us to have visual sensations in the mind. When we act voluntarily, acts of the will, which are forms of mental activity, cause physical changes in the brain, which cause the muscles to move.

However, given dualism, this two–way interaction between the mind and the brain is inexplicable. The substances mind and matter are utterly different in kind, and this makes interaction between them obscure, placing doubt on the whole idea of dualism. How does the mind control something that is physical, if it is not in itself physical?

This problem is more grave if the mind is a non-spatial entity, as Descartes claims. If the mind has no location in space, then it is wrong to imagine it close to or inside the brain. My mind is no closer to my brain than it is to the other side of the galaxy. Why, then, does it have a direct causal influence only on my brain? There seems to be no way of explaining why *my* mind does not cause movement in *your* body, or, come to that, in a planet the other side of the galaxy. If non–spatial acts of will cause changes in my brain, this must be a form of psychokinesis or magic. Why is only my brain affected by this psychokinesis? In brief, dualism cannot explain the causal connection between the mind and body. On the other hand, if the mind does exist in space, then it has a size and a location, and it ought to be publicly detectable by some form of observation, which it is not.

Furthermore, dualism seems to contradict neurology. When particular parts of the brain are destroyed, we lose specific mental capabilities. Substance dualism cannot explain this satisfactorily: if the mind and the body are two distinct substances, and if it is the mind that remembers, then it ought to be able to do this quite independently of what the brain does. However, in fact, when particular brain cells are killed, this will destroy particular memories (Churchland, 1988, p. 20). Dualism also contradicts the principle of the conservation of energy. According to physics, the material universe is a closed system in which total energy is conserved. If Descartes' view were right, then there would be physical changes in the brain that do not have a sufficient physical cause, and this would imply denying the conservation of energy. The principle of the conservation of energy is more than just a physical law. If the law of the conservation of energy were frequently violated, physics would be impossible, because the principle is a necessary condition for other particular physical laws, such as Force = mass times acceleration, or F=MA. If force were less than mass times acceleration, then mass could accelerate without sufficient force to cause it to do so. If, on the other hand, force were greater than mass times acceleration, then there would be force that is mysteriously lost without any physical effect. In other words, if the principle of the conservation of energy were false, then F would not equal MA. Similar arguments can be applied to other physical laws. In other words, the principle of the conservation of energy makes other physical laws possible. Therefore, the denial of the conservation of energy is an important objection against substance dualism.

2. The Problem of Identity

Two material objects that are otherwise identical (such as two hydrogen atoms) can be distinguished by their different positions in space at the same time. Objects are publicly identifiable by their spatio–temporal position. However, according to Descartes, minds do not have a spatial position, and thus there is no guarantee that we can publicly distinguish between two similar disembodied minds. This puts into question the thesis that the mind is a substance because substances must be publicly identifiable. If substances were not publicly identifiable, then there would be no clear sense or content to the claim that two people can refer to or talk about the same thing. To be referred to by public words, things must have public criteria of identity, and non-spatial minds do not satisfy this condition.

3. The problem of Other Minds

There are two problems for the dualist regarding other minds. The first problem is epistemological, concerning the knowledge of other minds: How can I know that other beings are conscious? If I am only acquainted with other people's behavior, how can I know that

64

there is a mind causing that behavior? For all I know, two or more mental substances might be causing the behavior of a person. Alternatively, it might have purely physical causes. In such a case, according to Descartes, the person could not be a conscious being at all, no matter how sophisticated or, like my own, his or her behavior was.

Furthermore, it would be absurd to suggest that I do not know whether others have feelings and thoughts, and yet Descartes' dualism does suggest this. It suggests this because it implies that behavior is logically irrelevant in settling the question as to whether others are conscious or not.

Dualism has another problem concerning other minds. On reflection, it is obvious that the word 'pain' has a public meaning; when I say 'I am in pain,' other English speakers understand me, and similarly, when other people tell me that they are in pain, I can understand them. Because we can understand each other, the word 'pain' has a shared meaning. The same applies to other words that describe our feelings and thoughts.

Dualism has difficulties accounting for the fact that words such as 'pain' have a public meaning. It treats mental states as purely private and subjective, and does not link them conceptually to any public and objective criteria, such as behavior. Consequently, it implies that I know the meaning of a word such as 'pain' only because of my own feelings of pain. It gives such words a purely phenomenological and private definition. This has the absurd consequence that other people may not mean the same by words such as 'pain' and 'anger' as I do, because each of us has our own definition. This makes understanding others impossible.

4. The Consciousness of Animals

Are birds conscious? Are they aware of the environment around them? Surely, they are. According to Descartes, only persons have souls or minds and, consequently, other creatures, such as birds, are not conscious. According to him, they are only complex machines. This presents the dualist with two problems.

First, if we can explain everything that a bird or a monkey can do without postulating a non-material mind, then surely the same applies to humans, especially babies. For example, it appears that it is possible to teach chimpanzees and gorillas sign language. The apes use the sign language in way that shows complex linguistic abilities, such as syntactical structure. There is a difference between, 'I hit you' and 'You hit me.' This difference is signified by the position of the words, which the apes are able to differentiate. Another characteristic of language is that we are able to use old words in new circumstances.

65

The monkeys and gorillas can do this. Not only can they use old worlds in new situations, but they can also create new words. For example, the gorilla Koko called a grapefruit a 'yellow orange.' Consider that monkeys and other animals show love to their families, and demonstrate complex feelings and visual abilities. If we can explain these capacities in the case of chimpanzees, without postulating a non-material soul, then we do not need to postulate it either for humans.

The second problem for the dualist is that the differences between we humans and the other animals are ones of degree, not ones of kind. A spider is less conscious than a bird. Yet a spider has quite sophisticated perceptions. This is more so for a bird, and even more so for a monkey. Consequently, consciousness is a matter of degree, and not one of kind. It is more like a dimmer than an on/off light switch. Descartes' theory cannot accommodate this continuous variation in the nature of consciousness. Descartes stated that consciousness is a simple property of a non-material mind. For the dualist, either an animal has or it does not have a mind or soul.

Materialism

Materialism is the view that only matter and its properties exist. This implies that non-material minds do not exist. Materialism presents us with the challenge of explaining how consciousness is possible in a purely material world (although, as we shall see, it does not solve that challenge, even if it is true). Materialism is often called the identity theory, because it claims that mental states are identical to brain states. We shall see that this way of expressing the position is misleading.

The arguments in favor of materialism are as follows. First, it is ontologically simpler than dualism. Since we should prefer simpler explanations, then if we do not need to postulate the existence of mental substances and properties, and can explain consciousness without them, it is preferable to exclude them from our theory of the mind. This argument does not seem to be decisive because it assumes that we can explain consciousness without the need for postulating mental entities, and this still remains to be shown.

A second argument in favor of materialism makes this last requirement more explicit. It claims that mental states are identified by their causal effect on the behavior and other mental states (Armstrong, 1968). According to the causal analysis, mental states are by definition whatever is capable of causing actions or appropriately complex behavior. Recent philosophers, such as David Armstrong, have appealed to neurological and physiological theory to argue that in fact all actions are caused solely by the functioning of the central nervous system or the brain. Armstrong concludes that mental states are brain states. His argument can be summarized as follows:

Argument 9

1. By definition, mental states are whatever is capable of causing intentional actions.
2. As a matter of fact, all intentional actions are caused solely by activity in the brain.
3. Therefore, mental states are brain states.

In short, by definition, a mental state is whatever has a certain causal role; but, as a matter of fact, the only thing that has that role is the brain and, therefore, mental states are brain states (see page 77).

Problems with Materialism

We have just described materialism as an identity claim: mental states are identical to brain states. This gives us a good clue as to how to argue against materialism. For if X and Y are identical, then everything that is true of X must be true of Y, and vice versa. To show the identity claim to be false, we must show that everything true of X is not true of Y, or vice versa. Let us look at some arguments based on this clue.

1) Suppose the materialist claims that the mind is identical to the brain. To show this to be false, we must think of some property that the mind has which the brain does not have. Apparently, this is easy. Go into the hospital pathology lab and take a specimen brain: a piece of raw, jelly-like meat. It is dead and, therefore it is not conscious, and therefore, it is not a mind. However, this is too simplistic a refutation of materialism. The materialist should not affirm that it is the brain that is identical to the mind. The brain per se is not the issue. It is the brain's functions. So, let us reformulate the identity thesis: mental states are brain states.

2) However, there is an argument against this revised claim. Sensations are mental states. My sensation is one of green, but there is nothing green about my brain and, therefore, this sensation is not a brain state. Consequently, materialism is a false theory of mind. The form of this argument is as follows:

Argument 10

1. There is a property that my sensation has which my brain state lacks.
2. If sensations and brain states are identical then they must have <u>the same properties.</u>
3. Therefore, the two cannot be identical.

This argument against materialism also fails. The materialist position was not carefully stated. Materialism should not treat sensations as things, i.e. it should not reify mental states. The materialist should not affirm: there is a thing called a sensation, or a thought, which is really a brain state. The above argument falsely assumes that this is what a materialist would claim. Therefore, the criticism succeeds only in showing that a carelessly worded materialist position is false.

Instead, the materialist should identify the *having of* particular sensations with the *having of* particular brain states. In other words, the materialist does not assert that mental states are brain states, but rather that *being in* a particular mental state is the same as *being in* a particular brain state.

3) This leads to another argument against materialism: general types of mental states, such as pain, cannot be identified with general types of brain states, such as the firing of neurons in the frontal lobe. Pain in you might have a different physical composition from pain in me, or from pain in a being from Venus. Consequently, we cannot identify general types of mental states with types of brain states.

Most materialists accept this point. In reply, they argue that the having of particular or token mental states is identical to the having of particular token brain states. This reply appeals to the distinction between types and tokens. A token is a particular example of some general sort or kind of thing or type. The following three inscriptions 'A A A' are three tokens of the one type, the letter 'A.' Given this distinction, the having of every particular or token mental state is identical with the having of a particular or token brain state, but we cannot make generalizations about such identities and frame them as type/type identities. Consequently, the objection does not succeed in showing that token/token identity materialist theory is mistaken.

Finally, we need to clarify a point concerning materialism. Water and H_2O are the same. However, the two words 'H_2O' and 'water' have different meanings or senses. To understand the former, you need to know chemical theory; for understanding the latter, you do not. They

Mind and Brain

have different senses, but nevertheless, they refer to the same thing. Two words with different senses can have the same reference. This idea is part of the basis of materialism. Phrases with quite different meanings can refer to the same events or facts. In particular, 'John is in brain-state XZY' and 'John is thinking about Mary' do not have the same meaning. Yet, they can be true in virtue of the same facts.

In conclusion, the major arguments in favor of dualism fail and the theory has serious problems. The major argument in favor of materialism is difficult to evaluate at this stage, because it requires the causal theory of mind, which we shall explain in the next chapter (see page 75). However, so far, the major arguments against materialism fail.

Is the Problem Ontological?

The debate between the dualist and the materialist is ontological. It concerns what exists. The materialist asserts that only matter exists and the dualist claims that non-material minds exist as well. But does either of these positions really solve the problem with which we started? The problem was how to reconcile materialistic science with our everyday conception of ourselves as conscious beings.

Reifying ideas and the mind, or treating them as entities does not explain how consciousness is possible. For instance, the following marks are written on the chalkboard: 'The cat sat on the mat.' These marks have meaning. To reify the meaning would be to claim that there are two entities involved here: the sentence written on the board, and the non-physical, ghostly entity called 'the meaning of the sentence.' When we physically change a word, we also change the non-physical aspect of the sentence. Does this explain how physical marks have meaning? No. In a similar way, both dualism and materialism try to tell us what exists, but neither explains what consciousness is. This does not mean that any one of the two theories is false, but it suggests that they are not directly relevant to the issue at hand.

Nevertheless, the example also suggests that we can free ourselves of a prejudice: namely,

P: matter cannot be conscious.

It is indeed puzzling how matter can be conscious. But it is equally puzzling how a non-material thing can be conscious. This is why P is a prejudice. It is an enigma how a material thing can be conscious, but it is equally mysterious how a non-material thing can be conscious.

Consider the last two minutes of a world cup soccer final. Let us describe exactly what happened in those two minutes when a certain team won with a last minute goal. The space used in a soccer game is limited. Furthermore, there are a limited number of different types of molecules involved in a game of soccer, such as those that constitute the leather of the ball, the skin and flesh of the players, their uniforms, the wood of the goal posts. Suppose that there are 1000 types of molecules involved in the game. We could describe the last two minutes of the game by describing the positions of all the different molecules at each moment of time. It would be a very long and boring description. Yet, in a sense, that is exactly what happened. The problem is that it does not tell you what is important about the game, such as who won and what tactics they used, and so on.

This, however, does not mean that we have left out the immaterial essence of soccer, the soul of the game. It does not imply that there is some non-material essence of the game that we have omitted from our long description. Let us call the purely molecular description EXT (for extensional). Now, consider the normal description of the game. It mentions who scored the goal etc. Let us call the normal description INT (for intensional). The mistaken idea that we have left out some important *thing* from our molecular description can be expressed with a formula:

$$INT = EXT + M$$

'M' stands for some magical *thing* that is the soul of the game. This is what we might call the dualist view of soccer.

This formula does not help us understand soccer. We do not need to posit some extra magical thing to describe the game properly. INT and EXT are simply two ways of describing the same game of soccer. They are descriptions of the same events using different terminology. It does not help our understanding to claim that the difference between the two is some magical element, M. Dualism does not solve the problem of the relation between INT and EXT.

This point also applies to language. By making some marks on the board, I wrote a meaningful sentence in English. The physical marks can be described in molecular terms. We can call this description EXT. It does not tell you the meaning of what I wrote. The description of what I meant, we can call INT. The dualist view of these two descriptions would be captured with the same formula:

$$INT = EXT + M.$$

Once again, this posits the existence of a non-material magical thing, the meaning of the sentence. However, this postulation does not explain how marks can mean anything. Rather, EXT and INT are two different types of description of the same thing. Adding in an extra thing, M, does not help our understanding.

With these examples, I am trying to show that dualism provides only the illusion of an explanation of how a person can be conscious. This illusion reinforces the prejudice that physical things cannot be conscious. The puzzle of consciousness applies equally to both brains and non-material minds. Thus, debating the ontological issue will not explain how awareness is possible.

We can see the same point in another, even more simple, way. Is a table more than a bunch of atoms? If you answer negatively that does not seem exactly right because, for a collection of atoms to be a table, they have to be highly organized. But the positive answer is not correct either: there is no additional thing involved. By distinguishing different uses of 'is,' we can easily solve this apparent problem. First, there is the 'is' of identity: for example, 'Jekyl is Hyde.' Second, there is the 'is' of composition, as in 'the table is a collection of atoms,' which tells you the constituents of something. A table is composed of nothing more than a bunch of atoms, in a highly organized form. However, the organization is not an additional constituent of the table. It is not a thing in addition to the atoms. We cannot explain how consciousness and mental states are possible by affirming and denying that a human being is made up of atoms. In the debate between the materialist and the dualist, the issue is merely in the composition of a person. Therefore, the question of consciousness is not solved ontologically.

Appendix: Life After Death

Suppose that there is a life after death. What would it be like? Our mental functions depend on the physical brain. For example, if I cut out a part of your brain, then you would not be able to speak. If I cut out another, then you will not be able to see. Another will destroy your memory. Death wipes out all of these mental functions at a stroke. Life after death would be like existing without a thought and without desire. It would be like pure silence.

Can I survive my death? The important word here is 'I.' Who am I? I am Garrett Thomson, but this way of referring to me seems to imply reference to my body, because others can refer to me in this way. If there is life after death, then what survives is not Garrett Thomson, this person with these memories and this body. If I am rendered paralyzed and vegetable-like after a car accident, in what sense have I survived? I cannot remember, see, hear, or think. I exist in the sense that this body, with this genetic code, continues to function. However, one cannot identify the person that might survive death by reference to the particular genetic code inherited from his or her parents, for that does not survive. Furthermore, my memories, desires and thoughts do not survive.

Can you imagine losing an arm? People who find it hard to reconcile themselves to such a loss sometimes feel phantom limbs. They experience an itch in the limb they have lost. Can you imagine losing all four limbs? Can you imagine losing your memory? The neurologist Oliver Sacks describes a man without a memory who constantly greets people as if he had meet them for the first time (Sacks, 1985). Death is at least the loss of the whole body and all the mental functions that make up everyday life. If it is more than that, then it is the end. In what sense do *you* survive death? What were you before your conception? Both questions stretch the word 'you' to the limit.

How old are you? Suppose you reply 'Twenty' (plus some or all of the nine months after conception but before birth). This answer implies that you did not exist before conception. If you are a soul that existed prior to conception, then you should not answer 'Twenty.' Perhaps, you should answer 'I am infinitely old.' What was life like before conception, without thoughts and desires, memories and wishes? It was like silence. In what sense was it *you*?

The term 'life after death' is paradoxical. If there is a life after death, then we should not call the death of the body, 'death.' If there was life before conception, then perhaps, we ought not refer to the conception of the body as 'conception.' The mystery is that if there is a life after death and prior to conception, then in what sense will it be *you* that survives?

Some people argue that the possibility of life after death implies that materialism is false. There are two interesting points here. First, for that argument to succeed, it assumes that what survives death is not made of matter. For example, some people claim that angels are made of light. This would mean that angels are not non-material beings. With the discovery of many strange kinds of sub-atomic particles, can you confidently assert that the soul is non-material? What does 'material' and 'non-material' mean anyway? This is not an easy question to answer. Puzzling over these questions emphasize the redundancy of the ontological debate. We cannot explain consciousness with either dualism or materialism alone. Second, the possibility of life after death does not vindicate traditionally conceived dualism. This is because the idea of what life after death might be like is radically altered by the knowledge that mental functions are neurologically based. Perhaps, it cannot be imagined except as a silence. Or perhaps, after all, death is simply the end.

7

Saving The Mental

Most mental states are intentional. This means that they are about something. Whenever one believes, thinks, or wants, such states are always directed towards something. For instance, one believes that P, and the proposition 'P' that follows the word 'that' specifies the propositional content of the mental state. Contrast this with physical states, such as being a certain weight. As such, they are non-intentional. They are not about anything, and do not have a content.

How should we characterize the content of mental states? This question is a way to examine the nature of the mind without concentrating on the ontological debate. We should try to answer the question without presupposing either dualism or materialism, since, as we saw in the previous chapter, neither adequately answer the question: How is consciousness possible? We need to move to another level.

In fact, there are two very different approaches to this kind of question regarding the content of mental states: the introspective model, and the causal or functionalist model of consciousness. This takes us to the second level in the mind-body debate. However, as we shall see later, the problem cannot be entirely solved even at this second level.

THE SECOND LEVEL: MENTAL CONTENTS

How are we to specify the intentional content of a mental state? Descartes assumed that the content of mental states should be defined and identified by how they feel, by the qualities they present directly to introspective consciousness. He expressed this by saying that an idea is essentially the immediate object of perception. Descartes claims that each individual knows the content of his or her mental states, because we directly experience them. He offers us an introspective model of consciousness, which claims that the contents of consciousness should be characterized directly in terms of how they feel to the person having the experience.

While Descartes' view accords with popular opinion, it has several difficulties. First, it assumes that mental states are transparent to the person having them. This appears to be true of some mental states, but not of others. For example, sometimes, we think that we are angry, when in fact we are sad. One can be frightened without realizing it and, sometimes, we want without knowing exactly what we want.

Furthermore, there are some dramatic cases of neurological disorders. In one example, a man goes to a neurologist and claims that he has lost his vision. The neurologist decides to perform tests on him. He presents the patient with different colored shapes and asks the patient to say what they are. The patient protests that he is blind, but the doctor insists that the patient should guess and the patient reluctantly agrees to do so. Despite his remonstrations that he cannot see, the patient answers correctly every time. In some sense, the patient is seeing without being aware that he is (Sacks, 1985).

Furthermore, the introspective theory faces the problem of other minds, which we examined in the previous chapter. It is possible to know what another person is thinking. Our everyday commerce relies on this mutual knowledge of each other's mental states. But Descartes' account apparently makes this impossible. Moreover, we use the same words to refer to our own mental states as we do to describe those of other people. The word 'pain' cannot have an essentially private meaning for me, to describe only the content of my own mental state, because I can use it to describe what others are feeling.

In view of these difficulties, philosophers in the twentieth century began to develop another conception of the content of mental states, as an alternative to Descartes'. The alternative is to think of the content of mental states causally, in terms of their possible effects on behavior or actions and their typical causes. In other words, to feel pain is to be in a state which would normally cause such and such behavior (e.g. how an angry people would normally behave if they are uninhibited). More

75

generally, a mental state is defined by its causal role: it is a primarily a dispositional state to behave in certain ways under certain conditions.

One of the strong features of this account is that it treats consciousness as complex. As we saw in the last chapter, Descartes regarded consciousness as a simple property, and this leads to difficulties in accounting for degrees of consciousness, or in allowing for the fact that a spider is less conscious than a rabbit. The causal theory can account for this more readily because, according to it, consciousness consists in a wide gamut of mental states and dispositions that should be analyzed functionally or causally. For example, seeing consists of the abilities to recognize a sphere from a cube, to differentiate different colors, to distinguish shade from light, to recognize edges and borders and so forth. In other words, in visual perception, any cognitive function has a range of sub-functions. We should not think of consciousness as a simple property, but as a range of different things that we can do.

We have two approaches to defining mental content: Descartes' introspective account, and the functional/causal model. A major difference between these is that, whereas the more contemporary functional/causal approach provides a public criteria for the differentiation and identification of mental states, the introspective approach provides an essentially first-person and subjective criterion. Looked at one way, this difference is a reason for thinking that the contemporary causal approach is preferable, since we can know that another person is in pain. However, with the causal approach, we appear to have lost what is essential to experience, its subjectivity or first-person character. If this is so, then it is a damning criticism, and we will return to this point later.

From Behaviorism to Functionalism

The behaviorist claims that mental states are behaviorally based. To the question 'What is a mental state?' he or she will reply that it is being disposed to behave in certain ways given certain sensory inputs. To be in pain is to be disposed to cry out, withdraw the painful part of the body (Ryle, 1949).

However, this definition is too simplistic. The connection between sensory input and behavioral output does not depend on one mental state alone. For example, on its own, the desire to drink does not result in the action of walking in a certain direction, because it also requires another mental state, namely the belief that the café is in that direction.

General functionalism acknowledges the need for such interconnections between mental states. What is a mental state? The functionalist will reply: 'A disposition to act and to have other mental states, given certain sensory inputs and other mental states.' Functionalism identifies mental states by their causal role, their causes and effects, including other mental states. For example, part of what it means to be angry is to be disposed to have angry thoughts. This is the main difference between functionalism and behaviorism.

The point of the functionalist analysis is to show that mental states should be defined objectively by their causal roles, especially in relation to potential behavior, while still recognizing the interdependence of different mental states. It avoids defining the content of mental states in purely subjective or introspective terms, but without falling prey to the problems of simplistic behaviorism.

Functionalists distinguish between, on the one hand, types of mental states (such as pain) defined in terms of their causal role, and on the other hand, the particular occupants of that role, such as the particular physical state that performs that role on a particular occasion. A functional state may have multiple realizations in different beings; pain in a human, a Martian and a whale will be realized by different token or particular physical states (see page 69).

Some writers treat functionalism as an ontological claim (see, for example, Churchland, 1988, Chapter 1). Strictly speaking, this is not correct. A dualist could be a functionalist, arguing, for example, that we should define the mental states of non-material minds in terms of their causal effects on behavior. In theory, a functionalist might claim that the mental states of non-material spirits and ghosts should be defined functionally or causally. However, in practice all functionalist are in fact materialists. Moreover, as we have seen, there is an argument in favor of materialism that uses as a premise the claim that mental states are defined by their causal role (see page 67). Nevertheless, functionalism makes dualism redundant, but not false.

The Private Language Argument Revisited

Is functionalism true? We have seen the strengths of the theory, but the nagging doubt remains that the functionalist or causal theory seems to leave out the most important aspect of experience, namely its subjectivity. Recently, some philosophers have argued that the functional/causal approach omits the essential subjectivity of experience, and cannot account for subjective facts, such as what it is like to be a bat or a whale (Nagel, 1979 and Searle, 1994, p.93).

What does this loss amount to? We have already seen that Wittgenstein's private language argument challenges Descartes' assumption that the immediate objects of perception are ideas in the mind (see page 55). It also challenges the claim that we can identify the content of our mental states directly in terms of how those states feel. If this challenge succeeds, then there can be no returning to Descartes' introspectivist position. In effect, Wittgenstein argues against the possibility of an essentially private language, which privately names different sensations (Wittgenstein, 1953). If such an essentially private language is impossible, then the essentially private identification of sensations and mental states is also impossible.

Normally, we identify mental states by their public causes and effects: for example, 'the feeling of having eaten too much.' This way of identifying sensations presupposes the existence of the external world, and hence is prohibited in Descartes' original position, in which the existence of the public world is in doubt. His original position requires an essentially private language that obtains its meaning directly by referring to the privately felt quality of sensations, without relying on external causal factors. Wittgenstein argues that such a language is impossible, and this means that it is impossible to identify sensations directly, contrary to what Descartes supposes.

If this argument is sound, then we cannot identify the content of our mental states directly in terms of how they feel. This does not imply rejecting subjectivity, but only a certain understanding of it. It means that the content of mental states cannot be identified in an essentially private manner, and instead, must be thought of in public terms, as the functionalist or causal theory insists. For instance, perceptions must be identified in terms of the external objects that typically cause them, such as the taste of cherries and the sound of rain, or in terms of the behavior they typically cause.

THE THIRD LEVEL: DESCRIPTIONS

Many people feel that materialism leaves out something vitally important, namely the human spirit. Contemplating a universe of particles in space-time, one is tempted to ask: 'Is that all there is?' Materialism apparently informs us that the universe is nothing but packets of energy crashing about without purpose and value. Contemplating a beautiful painting, one is inclined to ask the materialist: 'Do you mean that these exquisite feelings are nothing but electrical impulses in my brain?' (The reply should be 'no;' see page 68 below). Neurons fire and chemicals change, but none of this seems to include the feelings themselves. Materialism apparently banishes color and consciousness from the world.

However, these ways of expressing the concern take us straight back to the ontological issue, to level one. We already have seen that this is an unhelpful approach, and we should not want to return to

Descartes' dualism. Alternatively, we could try to express this concern at level two. We could argue that functionalism omits the all-important subjective aspect of experience. The problem is that this way of expressing the concern is frustrated by the private language argument. However, there is another way of dealing these worries, which does not require regressing to levels one and two. This takes us to the third level.

3.1 Two Different Types of Description

There are two fundamentally different ways of thinking about and describing a human being. We can describe a person in the extensional mode, for example, by stating his or her location and height, or by characterizing the individual's brain-state. Also we can characterize persons in the intensional mode, by describing how they feel, and what they think. What is the relation between these two types of description? More specifically, can the latter be reduced to the former?

What are extensional and intensional descriptions? In an extensional context, two phrases or words with the same reference can be substituted without changing the truth-value of the sentence as a whole (see page 61). For example, there is an indefinite number of ways of referring to Paul. He can be referred to as the only English person in the room, the only being who was such and such place at such and such time, or as the eldest son of Martha Travelli. In the sentence 'Paul is six feet tall,' we can substitute for 'Paul' any one of the phrases which uniquely refer to him, without changing the truth or falsity of the sentence as a whole. The sentence 'Paul is six feet tall' is extensional.

On the other hand, in an intensional sentence, words or phrases with the same reference cannot be so substituted. Consider the sentence 'Jennifer believes that Paul is tall.' This does not imply that Jennifer believes that the eldest son of Martha is tall. Even though Paul is Matha's eldest son, Jennifer might not know that, or she might fail to make the connection. 'Jennifer believes that...' forms an intensional or non-extensional context.

Psychological verbs followed by a 'that...' clause are typically all intensional or non-extensional For example, 'Jennifer wants that...' and 'Jennifer hopes that...' are intensional. The truth-value of the sentences formed by such phrases depends on how one describes the thing in question. Jennifer wants X under one description, but does not want the same thing under another. Frank believes that P, but not that Q, even though P is equivalent to Q. Such sentences are non-extensional.

We should not confuse intensionality (with an 's') and intentionality (with a 't'). They are distinct concepts, even though they are linked. Intentionality is a feature of mental states, namely their characteristic of aboutness, which we discussed at the beginning of this chapter. On the other hand, as we have just seen, intensionality is a feature of some sentences. Intensional sentences, such as 'Jennifer believes that Paul is tall,' are those in which a word or phrase cannot be replaced by another word or phrase with same reference without possibly changing the truth of the sentence as a whole. This is the difference between the two notions. At level 2, we discussed intentionality (with a 't'); now, at level 3, we are examining intensionality (with an 's').

However, the two notions are intimately related because the intensionality of a sentence is a linguistic reflection of something having intentional content. Intensionality is a mirror of intentionality. The intentionality of mental states is expressed by sentences that specify their content, such as 'Jennifer believes that...' These sentences have a 'that' clause and what follows the 'that' clause specifies the content of the mental-state. This clause makes the sentence intensional.

With these clarifications in hand, we can return to the original question. A person can be described in extensional terms. For instance, 'Jennifer is six and a half feet tall' and 'Jennifer's brain is undergoing intense electrochemical activity in the frontal lobe' are extensional sentences. The descriptions of a person provided by the physical sciences are typically extensional. However, a person also can be described in intensional terms, as a person with thoughts and feelings. Psychological descriptions, such as 'Jennifer thinks that she will win' are intensional. Are intensional description based on extensional ones? Can the one be reduced to the other?

Such questions are not ontological and this is why level 1 is distinct from level 3. Dualism and materialism are ontological claims concerning the kinds of things that exist, or about the composition of the universe. The questions we are now asking are not of that type. Suppose materialism is true, dualism is false, and a person is a physical thing. This does not exclude the possibility of giving true intensional descriptions of a person. Denying the mind as a non-physical entity does not banish psychological or intensional descriptions of persons. On the other hand, suppose that dualism is true, that materialism is false, and there are non-physical entities. This does not exclude the possibility of giving extensional descriptions of such entities. The two issues are distinct. Whereas ontology is concerned with what exists, the point we are examining now concerns what kinds of descriptions we can give of what exists.

Given these explanations, we can now recast the question of how to conceive of the mind's place in nature. Scientific descriptions of the physical universe are extensional sentences and our everyday psychological descriptions of ourselves are intensional. The negative point made at the end of the previous chapter that the mind/body riddle is not primarily ontological may be replaced by the more positive suggestion that the problem concerns the relationship between intensional and extensional descriptions. The enigma is not 'What are we composed of?' but rather 'How may we be truly described?'

3.2 The Three Strategies

In part, the problem of how consciousness is possible in a physical world can now be reformulated as: 'How can there be true intensional sentences when the universe can be characterized entirely extensionally?' Much contemporary debate in the philosophy of mind has revolved around three broad strategies to answer this question.

1) The first strategy is to reify the intensional or, in other words, to treat this mode of discourse as if it were about its own distinct realm of substances. We have already rejected this approach, because it regards the problem ontologically, which we argued is a fruitless exercise. It leads to dualism that explains nothing. It takes us back to level one.

2) The second strategy is to claim that intensional sentences can be reduced to extensional ones. This is sometimes called 'reductive materialism.' The reductive materialist claims that sentences such as 'Martha believes that Paul is tall' can be reduced without remainder into extensional sentences about John's brain states.

3) The third strategy is to argue that the universe can be characterized completely without intensional descriptions and, therefore, the intensional mode can be eliminated. This is sometimes called 'eliminative materialism.' The eliminative materialist rejects the claim that such sentences can be reduced to extensional ones, but insists that intensional sentences in principle can be dropped out of a complete true description of the world, including human beings.

The terms 'reductive and eliminative materialism' are misleading, despite their use in the philosophical literature (see Churchland, Ch, 2, Sections 3 and 5). They suggest that reductionism and eliminativism are ontological claims about mental states. However, since materialism already denies the existence of distinct mental states and substances, this cannot be right. According to materialism, there are no such entities or states to be eliminated or reduced. In fact, eliminativism and reductionism are claims about language or sentences, rather than things.

They are theories concerned with the relation between the extensional and intensional descriptions of animate beings.

These are deep waters. They flow back to the concerns that motivated Descartes, namely our view of ourselves in a scientifically described universe. The physical sciences can be characterized in purely extensional terms. Consequently, it seems that, if psychological descriptions are to fit into the physical sciences, then psychological, intensional characterizations have to be reducible to extensional ones. Can the psychological, which must be described intensionally, be characterized within the constraints of physical scientific theory, which is extensional? This seems to depend on whether the intensional can be reduced to the extensional.

3.3 The First Strategy: Reification

Expressions such as 'the desire for food,' or 'the belief he had,' or 'the mind,' apparently function like names that refer to things. Because of this, we are led uncritically to believe that such phrases must name mental entities. For example, 'The politician would not give up his belief' seems to imply that the politician possesses a belief, similar to the way in which a person owns a car. The same point applies to terms such as 'sensation,' 'the will,' 'consciousness,' and 'decision.' If we fall into the trap of thinking that the noun 'belief' refers to a thing, namely a belief, then we will puzzle what such a mental object could be.

The initial assumption, namely that all nouns must name things, is false. To avoid the problems inherent in this assumption, we could treat for instance the verb form 'believes' as primary compared to the noun 'the belief.' We could replace 'I have the belief that P' with 'I believe that P,' and 'I have the sensation of red' with 'I see red.' The verb 'to believe' reifies less than the noun 'the belief.'

This type of approach avoids some of the difficulties inherent in the position of the empiricists and Descartes, who tend to reify ideas. Their claim that we can only directly perceive our own ideas leads to the fatal question: 'How can we know that these ideas truly represent things in the external world?' It brings the problem of how we can know external objects that are hidden behind the veil of ideas. However, once we stop reifying ideas, and give up the assumption that they are all we can perceive, then we may admit that we can directly see, smell, and touch physical objects. In short, reifying leads to a mistaken theory of perception. Furthermore, reifying consciousness and mental-states as if they were objects leads to dualism, returning us to level one.

3.4 The Second Strategy: Reduction

The second strategy argues that intensional descriptions of psychological states can be reduced to extensional descriptions of brain states. As a first shot, we may define 'reduction' as follows: a sentence reduces to another when the second entails the first. For example, the sentence 'the average person in the world earns $700 per annum' reduces to a set of sentences about the earnings of each individual in each country, the statement that there are no other people and the mathematical definition of 'average.' This latter set of sentences entails the first. A more complete scientific definition of reduction is the following. A theory T2 is reducible to theory T1, when the laws of T2 are logically derivable from those of T1, given certain bridge principles, either causally or definitionally connecting the expressions of T2 with those of T1 (Nagel, 1961, Ch. 11 and Kim, 1996, Ch. 9).

Please note that the issue is not whether we can reduce mental states to physical states. Since materialists already claim that being in a token mental state is identical to being in a token brain state, this way of explaining reduction confuses reductionism with materialism. Reduction is not ontological. It concerns the relation between sentences or descriptions. Consequently, the reductionist thesis should be distinguished from ontological materialism, the claim that only physical objects exist. An ontological materialist could reject the assertion that all intensional descriptions are reducible to extensional ones. Materialism does not force us to be reductionist.

Many philosophers think that the prospects for such a reduction are bleak, because of the difficulty (or perhaps impossibility) of finding appropriate bridge principles (see Davidson, 1980). No set of physical descriptions will imply an intensional description, because the intensional mode utilizes concepts that are richer or thicker than those used by the extensional and which cannot be derived from the latter. Furthermore, no intentional description will imply a particular physical one, because the intentional could be realized in many different physical ways, as the token identity theory of materialism recognizes.

If intensional sentences cannot be reduced to extensional ones, this means that psychological statements cannot be incorporated into the language of physical science. This view presents a problem for those who want to unify everyday statements about people's mental states with the physical sciences. Some philosophers argue that this is a reason for being suspicious about the credentials of everyday folk psychology.

3.5 The Third Strategy: Eliminativism

According to eliminativism, the intensional concepts with which we describe people's psychological states are inherently confused and vague. For example, a dog scratches and whines at the closed door. At first, we might claim 'He believes that his owner is in the room.' However, after reflection, we may deny that the dog really has the concepts of a master and of a room. Another example, it takes years to learn the theory of relativity. A child learns at school that space is curved but, of course, he cannot explain it, only repeat the formula. Should we say that he believes it? Similar points apply to other psychological concepts, such as desire, hope, wish and fear. According to eliminativism, such concepts are inherently vague and, for this reason, they will have to be replaced by the more precise scientific concepts of neuroscience (Stich, 1983, Ch. 5).

Please note that we should not confuse materialism, which is an ontological claim, with eliminativism, which is an assertion about intensional descriptions. Materialism merely asserts that there exists nothing in addition to matter. The stronger eliminativist claim concerns intensional descriptions, claiming that they are all false, and should be eliminated. For example, according to eliminativism, the statement 'George wants to swim' is strictly speaking false, not because George does not want to swim, but because the concept of wanting is inadequate in the ways described earlier. According to the eliminativist, eventually neurophysiology will replace psychological statements or folk psychology. A true description of the world will not include any intensional sentences.

The Californian philosopher Paul Churchland, who is an eliminativist, argues that neurologists should give up the attempt to make neurological explanations map onto ordinary psychology (Churchland, p. 47). He claims that it is probable that folk psychology is 'simply mistaken.' To argue his case, Churchland urges a historical comparison between the theory of phlogiston and everyday psychology. Phlogiston was thought to be a spirit-like substance released when things are burned. Churchland says:

> Phlogiston emerged, not as an incomplete description of what was going on, but as a radical misdescription ... the concepts of folk psychology - belief, desire, fear, sensation, pain, joy, and so on - await a similar fate (Churchland, p. 44).

To evaluate these claims, we should ask: 'Is folk psychology a theory, akin to scientific theories, as Churchland assumes?' If it is, then is it in competition with, and can it eventually be replaced by, neuroscience? If not, then what is it?

Folk psychology would not be a scientific theory if no empirical evidence could count against it. Compare it to our characterization of the physical world in terms of material objects. Some philosophers argue that 'material objects exist' is not a theoretical claim, because no evidence possibly could count against it. All empirical evidence presupposes it. What evidence could there be that material objects do not exist? Quantum mechanics is an extremely well verified theory, which might be a candidate for such evidence. It tells us that matter is constituted by probability wave functions, which do not have a specific location at any time. It apparently implies that the real world does not consist of solid three-dimensional objects at all.

However, I shall argue tentatively and briefly that ordinary object-discourse is not refuted by quantum mechanics, even if our conception of a material object is unclear. First, we should not take quantum mechanics to demonstrate that our belief in the existence of ordinary objects is false, but rather it shows us what such objects are composed of. Quantum mechanics gives us new and strange mathematical descriptions of the composition of such objects, but it does not eliminate talk of such objects because quantum mechanics presupposes ordinary object-discourse, for instance when the physicist reads his or her measurement apparatus. Second, we could not abandon talk of tables, rivers and housing estates in favor of quantum mechanical descriptions, because the two kinds of descriptions serve quite different functions and interests. As a consequence, the claim that material objects exist is not an empirical theory, because a theory is a set of statements that can be given up in the light of contrary empirical evidence. Ordinary object-discourse is more basic than any scientific theory. Such theories presuppose it.

With this analogy in mind, is folk psychology a theory? If it is not, then it is not in competition with neuroscience, and the basic assumption of eliminativism is false. First, let us be clearer what so-called 'folk psychology' actually is. The term can mislead us. Eliminativism should be committed to the purging of all intensional descriptions; remember that it is not an ontological position. This exorcism also should include characterizations of actions as such. The eradication of desire and belief descriptions would entail the removal of action-descriptions too, because the concepts of action, belief and desire form a triad. Typically actions are caused by desires and beliefs and must be described intensionally. For example, consider the sentence 'He turned on the light.' Even if this action caused the visitor to be electrocuted, you cannot conclude that 'He electrocuted the visitor' is a true description of his intentional action as such. In this way, actions are described as such with intensional sentences. Consequently, eliminativism is committed to the assertion that all intensional characterizations of actions are false and that the notion of an action should be also purged.

Folk psychology is not a theory, because no empirical evidence could possibly count against the claim that persons perform actions. A group of scientists could not gather evidence against the claim that persons perform actions, because gathering evidence is an action. They could not show us that no one ever performs an action, because such showing itself is an action. In this way, our everyday intensional ascriptions of belief, desire and actions are akin to the status of material object-discourse. Neither are empirical theories and they serve quite different functions from any empirical scientific theory. This is why the historical analogy that Churchland offers us, between folk psychology and the theory of phlogiston, fails. A more apt comparison would be between folk psychology and the belief that objects exist. Just as this belief is not threatened by quantum mechanics, neurology does not endanger our ascriptions of beliefs, desires and actions to persons.

3.6 Conclusions

How can there be true intensional descriptions in an extensionally characterized universe? This question is equivalent to asking how our normal psychological descriptions of ourselves can be fitted into the extensional scientific picture of the world. It gets us to the root of the problem that motivated Descartes, but without ensnarling us in misleading ontological questions at level one.

We have rejected the three most common strategies for dealing with this question: reification, reduction and elimination. Where does this leave us? It transforms the landscape by opening new possibilities. It enables us to embrace materialism and a functional or causal theory of the mind, and yet reject reductionism and eliminativism. In this transformed landscape, we can explain the feeling that something is left out of the materialist and causal accounts, without rejecting them, and without regressing to the discussions of levels one and two.

Both reductionism and eliminativism make the usually implicit assumption that only extensional descriptions characterize reality as it really is. They assume that intensional descriptions do not. Reductionism tries to salvage the intensional mode by arguing that it can be reduced to the extensional. Eliminativism argues that, since the intensional mode cannot be reduced, it must be scrapped.

Having rejected these two strategies, we must challenge the starting premise that only the extensional idiom of science describes reality as it really is. The alternative is to take the intensional and extensional modes more like equal partners, each of which serve different functions in describing reality. According to this option, these are two different types of description of human beings, which have different meanings. One does not reduce to the other and neither can be eliminated in favor of the other, but they may be true in virtue of the same states of affairs or events.

This position means that we are not forced to opt for any one of the three strategies. We can repudiate the assumption that, to avoid reifying mental states, one must reduce or eliminate intensional specifications of their content. We are not forced into the idea that to avoid reifying, we must reduce or eliminate.

How does this explain the feeling that materialism and functionalism leave something out, without regressing to the debates of levels one and two? An extensional characterization of the universe as a whole, as given by physical theory, would be a complete description of the universe, because it does not leave out any entity or thing. However, it is incomplete in the sense that there are plenty of other more interesting ways of truly characterizing things. In particular, we can truly describe what people think, want, and do in the intensional mode. Matter can be truly characterized in intensional terms when it is appropriately and sufficiently organized. Consequently, the extensional description of the whole universe is incomplete, in the sense that it does not include all true sentences.

In this sense, eliminativism and reductionism do leave something out, but without leaving some *thing* out. They reject the integrity of the intensional mode, by presupposing that such descriptions have to be reduced or eliminated. However, as we have seen, materialism and functional or causal theory need not be committed to reductive and eliminative strategies. Consequently, the feeling that materialism and functionalism omit something is based on confusing both with eliminativism and reductionism, which do. Furthermore, the rejection of eliminativism and reductionism does not vindicate Descartes. It does not imply that materialism and the causal account are false. One could argue in favor of materialism and functional or causal account at levels one and two, but reject reduction and eliminativism at level three.

Bringing Together the Three Levels

First, we have seen that the problem of the mind's place in nature is not primarily ontological. This insight took us to the second level. Mental states are intentional because they have propositional content, and this content should be thought of functionally, in terms of the

87

causal role of the mental states. This requires rejecting Descartes' view that the content of mental states should be specified through their introspective feel.

Some philosophers are uncomfortable with this rejection, because it seems to omit the subjective character of mental states. However, this thought seems to be negated by the private language argument, and there seems to be no cogent way of expressing the concern at the second level, and this point takes us to the third level.

At the third level, we can approach the puzzle of the mind through the contrast between intensional and extensional descriptions, characterizations of psychological states as such, and physical states as such. The puzzle is: 'How can there be true intensional statements in an extensionally characterized universe?' We have seen how at this level, we can vindicate the feeling that something has been left out, by arguing that eliminativism and reductionism are false.

8

The Dot Problem: Science

According to standard physical theory, there are only two types of particles: leptons and quarks. There are six kinds of each of these two particle-types. Leptons are light particles, which include the electron. Quarks are the constituents of the heavier hadron particles, which include protons and neutrons. Until recently, it was thought that there were four fundamental forces: gravity, electro-magnetic, and the weak and strong nuclear forces but, recently, the last three have been reduced to one. Thus, there are twelve types of particle and the two types of force. According to physical theory, nothing else exists except those things listed by this theory (Morris, 1990).

Furthermore, let us assume that there is a minimum space-time dot or granule smaller than which it is physically impossible for us to describe. This is roughly 3×10 to the power of minus 36 seconds and 10 to the power of minus 35 meters. Assume that the universe is 20 billion years old. Ignoring the fact that the universe has expanded, we can calculate that roughly there are 10 to the power of 227,035 space-time granules in the universe. The calculation is given in the appendix to this chapter.

To keep it very simple, let us assume that each one of those space-time dots or granules can have thirteen values (twelve corresponding to the particle types and one corresponding to nothing). According to physical theory, if we made a list of the actual value for

89

each of the space-time dots, then we would have a complete description of the universe. To give such a description would be physically impossible, because this number (10 to the power of 227,035) is so immense that not enough time has elapsed since the big bang to actually state such a description. (Actually, the description would have to be a lot more complicated because we would have to introduce the fundamental properties of each particle, describe the occupant of each granule in probabilistic terms, and take into account virtual particles that constitute the forces, and anti-particles. Furthermore, we would have to take into account non-local effects).

The Problem

Complications aside, would this really be a complete description of the universe? If the physical theory is right, then there is literally nothing else - no additional items that we have left off our list.

Physical theory appears to challenge our ordinary descriptions of the world. For example, our view of the universe must include room for language, and language requires the idea of meaning. How can meaning, metaphor and poetry be compatible with the statement that the quantum-dot description is complete?

Consider another example: we give evaluative descriptions of situations. We make claims such as: 'The room is dirty,' 'The action will lead to his ruin,' and 'My friend is generous.' Such statements appear to be true or false descriptions. Yet, at the same time, they appear to be evaluative: they involve appeal to norms or values. How can such descriptions be possible in a universe that is completely characterized by the dot description? This problem affects more than just morality, because not all evaluations are moral. We would like to think that we live in a beautiful, interesting and meaningful world; yet these hopes seem to be dashed to the ground by the dot theory.

We inhabit a world that appears to be much richer than the dots would allow. The universe apparently contains facts such as people getting angry, and companies selling services across national borders. We live in a world in which a poem can express an insight, a metaphor can convey a wealth of meaning, and in which work can be boring, especially on Friday. This seems to be a quite different universe from the dot one. But is it? Please note that the point of this chapter is not to argue that materialism is a true theory, but rather to show how our richer descriptions of the world might be compatible with it.

Reformulating the Problem

Actually, we already have the tools to help resolve these problems. These questions were answered indirectly in the previous chapter. The elements are already on hand. It is a matter of applying the lesson to new areas and reinforcing them.

In the previous chapter, we saw that there are three strategies for dealing with the relation between the extensional descriptions of neuroscience, and the intensional descriptions that characterize the content of mental states. We face the same problem once again. This is because characterizations of the meaning of language and evaluative descriptions also involve intensionality. Let us see why.

The claim 'Sentence S means that P' is directly intensional. To see this, suppose S is 'Garrett's father is bald' and P is 'Garrett's male parent is bald.' S does mean that P. Suppose that P is equivalent to Q, where Q stands for 'The only psychologist in Wislow is bald.' (My father happens to be the only psychologist in Wislow). If 'S means that P' were extensional, then we could substitute Q for P, without changing the truth-value of the whole sentence. That is what extensionality is (see page 79). However, if we make that substitution, the whole sentence becomes false, because 'Garrett's father is bald' does not have the same meaning as 'The only psychologist in Wislow is bald.' Consequently, sentences of the form 'S means that P' are intensional. In other words, the following is not a valid argument form:

1. S means that P.
2. <u>P is equivalent to Q.</u>
3. Therefore, S means that Q.

Many of the interesting descriptions we give of the world are intensional. Yet, scientific descriptions are extensional. Why is this? Typically intensional sentences specify content. For example, 'The sentence "Il pleut' means that it is raining' specifies the content of the original French sentence. 'John believes that water is a liquid' specifies the content of his belief. Because they specify content, intensional sentences reflect points of view on the universe. Consider John's belief: if we said 'John believes that H_2O is a liquid at room temperature' then, so to speak, we would be putting words into his mouth. That was not the content of his belief, which concerned water rather than H_2O. We have to express his belief in a way that correctly expresses his point of view; otherwise the statement of his belief will be false.

On the other hand, extensional sentences do not express a point of view. If true, then they are true, not from a specific point of view, but from any point of view. This is because, in an extensional sentence, coextensive terms may be substituted while preserving the truth-value of the sentence as a whole. With an extensional sentence, it does not matter from what point of view you consider it: if it is true, then it is true from any point of view. This is why scientific theories should normally be explained in extensional terms. At least according to the conventional view, the aim of such theories is to tell us how things are independently of any particular points of view.

A Solution: the Fourth Way

Scientific descriptions are extensional, but the descriptions of the world that engage and describe our concerns and interests, are intensional. In the previous chapter, we saw three strategies for conceiving the relation between them: reifying, reducing and eliminating the intensional (see page 80).

The first strategy affirms that intensional descriptions are true or false in virtue of non-material objects. In addition to matter, there also exist minds, ideas, meanings, and values. In other words, according to this first strategy, physical theory is mistaken. However, as we saw in the previous two chapters, this ontological extravagance is highly problematic, and does not solve the relevant problems. It does not answer questions such as: 'How is consciousness possible?' and 'How can marks on paper be sentences?' The magical element, M, referred to in Chapter 6, is no answer (see page 70).

Philosophers have developed the second and third strategies to avoid the first. The idea is that a universe containing intensional items contradicts physical science, and so, to avoid this, we need either to reduce or eliminate intensionality. However, this important idea is mistaken in two ways.

First, neither the eliminativist nor the reductionist strategies work. We cannot reduce intensional descriptions to extensional ones. Nor can we eliminate the intensional. The dot-description of the universe tells us nothing about what sentences mean, and what people want to say. Consequently, it cannot tell us even what the eliminativist wants to say by affirming his or her theory. Stating and understanding the eliminativist theory requires that the theory is false. Consequently, it fails. In summary, the three theories (eliminativism, reductionism and reification) are false.

Second, and this is the crucial point, we do not need to reduce or eliminate intensional sentences in order to avoid reifying the intensional. The idea that we must eliminate or reduce to avoid an ontological bulge and to be consistent with science is false. We can deny all three strategies. Let us call this rejection 'the fourth way.'

Despite the fact that the idea behind the fourth way is simple, it has important implications: we repudiate reification and thereby save science; we deny reduction and elimination and, thereby, save ordinary everyday life.

The fourth way denies the assumption implicit in reductionism and eliminativism that only extensional sentences describe reality as it really is. It asserts that intensional descriptions do so as well, but without reifying the intensional. The intensional and extensional modes both describe the same one reality, but do so in very different ways. For example, we can describe the marks on the board extensionally, in terms of dots or, intensionally, as a meaningful sentence. We can characterize the events of last night in terms of dots, or, intensionally, as a murder. There is plenty of room for many different kinds of descriptions of reality, so long as they are not contradictory.

However, the fourth way has an important requirement. We have to assert that the intensional descriptions and the dot-characterizations are true in virtue of the same states of affairs. Without this requirement, we fall back into dualism. The fourth way would become a form of dualism, incompatible with physical theory. We will come back to this point in the next section.

What does the fourth way imply for physical theory? Let us return to the universe of extensionally characterized dots. According to a simplified version of physical theory, this would be a complete characterization of the universe. The fourth way does not contradict that assertion, because the physical description does not leave out any *thing*. It does not omit additional non-physical entities, such as minds, meanings or values, because there are none. In this way, the dot-characterization is complete. It does not leave out any *thing*.

However, it is not complete in the sense that there is nothing else to say about the universe (and segments of it). There are plenty of other more engaging ways of truly characterizing segments of the universe. In particular,

• In everyday psychology, we can characterize what people think and want, in the intensional mode, without presupposing that such descriptions have to be reduced, or that they require postulating the existence of strange intensional things, namely minds.

• In everyday linguistics, we can describe what people, and what the sentences they write and speak mean, in the intensional mode, again, without assuming that such descriptions have to be reduced or that they require postulating the existence of strange intensional things, namely meanings or senses.

• With everyday evaluations, we can describe actions as harmful or oppressive, beneficial or liberating, in the intensional mode, once again, without assuming that these have to be reduced or that they require reifying strange intensional things, namely values.

Matter can be truly described in intensional terms, when it is appropriately and sufficiently organized. Thus, the extensional-dot description is incomplete, because it does not include all true sentences.

Once we reject the fundamental assumption that only extensional descriptions can characterize reality as it really is, then we can give up the assumption that the intensional mode of discourse has to be either reified, or reduced or eliminated. To avoid reifying, we do not have to reduce or eliminate. In which case, we are free of the theoretical pressure to opt for one of these three alternatives. According to the fourth way, we are not forced into the idea that to avoid reifying, we must reduce or eliminate.

How can there be linguistic meaning in a physical universe of dots? If we take this question ontologically, the answer is that there cannot. A physical universe excludes meanings or senses as intensional objects. At the same time, we can interpret this question non-ontologically to mean 'How can there be true intensional descriptions of physical things?' When the question is taken in this way, the answer is surprisingly simple: fundamentally, there is no obstacle; appropriately organized matter can be described in such terms, without the need to resort to the reductive or eliminative strategies. The solution is seen in the vanishing of the problem (Wittgenstein, 1998, prop. 6.521).

Similarly, how can there be value in a physical universe of dots? If this question means 'How can there be such *things* as values in a physical universe?' then the answer is that there cannot. In a completely physical universe, there are no such things as values. However, this does not preclude evaluative descriptions being true of segments of the universe. An event can be truly described as a triumph or as a disaster. We can give true intensional descriptions of a universe of dots, without accepting that such descriptions must be reified, reduced, or eliminated.

Two Challenges

This reply appears satisfactory. It allows to keep the ontology of physical theory and to avoid dualism. It avoids affirming that there are such non-material *things* as minds, values, and meanings. Yet, at the same time, by rejecting reductionism and eliminativism, it preserves

94

the integrity of descriptions other than the dot ones. It allows us to claim that richer, non-extensional descriptions of the world are possible.

How does it do that? By saying that we can have different kinds of descriptions of the same bits of matter. We can truly describe matter in the intensional mode. This reply is made possible by a simple distinction, which we saw in Chapter 6: meaning and reference. Two phrases or words, such as 'water' and 'H$_2$O,' can have the same reference, but different meanings. Similarly, two sentences can have different meanings, and yet they can be true in virtue of the same states of affairs or events. For example, consider the last two minutes of the world cup final discussed in Chapter 6 (see page 70).

We will examine now two challenges to this view. The first comes from a dualist, arguing that the fourth way is really a disguised form of dualism. The second objection argues that it is really a disguised form of reductive materialism.

The First Challenge: Dualism

How is the fourth way different from a sophisticated form of dualism? Not all dualists assert the existence of non-material things or substances, as Descartes did (see page 59). A sophisticated dualist could affirm that only material things exist, but that the universe consists of at least two kinds of facts: physical and psychological facts. According to this sophisticated form of dualism, all things are material, but not all facts are.

How is the position we have advocated different from this form of dualism? Certainly the two positions have a lot in common: in particular, the denial of the existence of non-material things. However, there does appear to be a difference.

What we have proposed is not a dualism of facts, but rather a dualism of descriptions. We have claimed that the same facts or events can be described, in some cases, in two ways: intensionally and extensionally. For example, some long extensional description of John's neurological state and an intensional description of his psychological state are true in virtue of the same facts. This is a dualism of descriptions and not of facts.

However, what does this difference amount to? The reply depends on what a fact is. What counts as the same or different facts? For example, consider 'John has only two brothers,' 'John has no sisters,' 'John's parents have only three male children.' Are these sentences true by virtue of the same fact? Or, do they describe different facts?

We can contrast two broad views of what constitutes a fact. According to the soft view, facts are linguistically determined. They are

95

like the ontological shadow of true sentences. In other words, for every single true sentence, there corresponds a different fact. Facts are quasi-linguistic: they can only be identified and individuated by true sentences. Consequently, there is no difference in extension between facts and true descriptions: for every true description, there is a fact. Therefore, on the soft view of facts, the fourth way and fact-dualism are essentially similar. This means that, on this view, the fourth way is a kind of sophisticated dualism.

On the other hand, according to the hard view of facts, facts are not quasi-linguistic. They are part of the world and, therefore, we should reject the formula that, for every true sentence, there corresponds a different fact. Different sentences could be true in virtue of the same fact. According to this view, the fourth way is not a form of fact-dualism, because we can distinguish, in extension, between facts and true descriptions.

Of course, this clarification does not tell us how, from the point of view of the hard theory, facts should be identified and individuated. It does not give us a positive theory to replace the soft view, but that is a different and difficult story. However, it allows us to conclude the following: given the soft view of facts, the fourth way is a form of fact-dualism. Given the hard view, it is not.

The Second Challenge: Reductive Materialism

The materialist says, 'Surely, the dot descriptions are more basic than the other intensional descriptions. This appears to be something you have denied, but which is true, because that is how reality is and other richer descriptions are true by virtue of how the dots are organized. In other words, we can explain these other descriptions in terms of the dots. Therefore, your position is really a form of reductive materialism.'

In reply to this, there are three points.

1) First, suppose the idea is that only the dot descriptions characterize reality as it is. If this were case, we would have to deny that intensional descriptions do so as well. Then, we would be back in the position of having to argue for eliminativism and reductionism, which are not viable theories. Taken in this sense, the objection fails.

2) Second, suppose the idea is that we can explain the intensional in extensional terms. But can we? For example, actions are typically explained intensionally, in terms of the desires and beliefs that cause them. Even if we suppose that there is an underlying physical causal mechanism in such cases, this still does not mean that we are

explaining the mental or an action (intensionally described) in extensional terms. Instead, we might be explaining the action as such in terms of beliefs and desires and explaining the action, described extensionally as a set of physical changes, in neurological terms. Furthermore, even if we grant that the mental can be explained in extensional terms, this does not necessarily mean that such an explanation amounts to a reduction. In other words, physical explanations may be in some sense more basic, without it being true that intensional sentences can be reduced to extensional ones.

3) Third, suppose the idea is that intensional and extensional descriptions are true by virtue of the same states of affairs. This is exactly what we have been saying. This still allows us to affirm that the latter are more basic than the former, but only in the following way: the mental (or the evaluative or the linguistic) is supervenient on the physical. The idea of supervenience is that one set of descriptions underlies another. Supervenience is usually defined as follows:

> Properties of type A are supervenient on properties of type B if and only if two objects cannot differ with respect to their A-properties without also differing with respect to their B-properties (Audi, 1996, p. 778).

For example, token descriptions of a person's psychological states supervene on token descriptions of their neurological states because any change in the former must be accompanied by a change in the latter. This does not mean that the former can be explained in terms of the latter nor reduced to them. It gives sense to the idea that one set of descriptions can be more basic than another, but without appealing to the idea of reduction.

The Other Sciences

The claim that physical theory is a complete description of the universe seems problematic for another reason. Where does it leave the other sciences? Suppose that we can organize the sciences as follows:

Social sciences
Psychology
Macro-biology
Micro-biology
Chemistry
Macro-physics

Quantum Mechanics

Does the claim that the dot description of the universe is complete imply that all these other sciences must be reducible to quantum mechanics? How are the other sciences possible in a universe of dots? Physical theory tells us that only the dots exist, but other sciences tell us that other things exist as well: atoms, molecules, cells, organisms, persons and societies. The problem is that we appear to have a contradiction between:

1. Only quantum dots exist
2. Atoms exist

These two sentences may appear contradictory. For example, if we claimed that atoms exist in addition to the quantum dots, then statement 1) would be false. However, the problem disappears when we consider that statement 3) is also true.

3. Atoms are composed only of quantum dots

In other words, when we assert that atoms, molecules and cells exist, we are not affirming that they exist in addition to the dots, because they are composed nothing except the dots. Physical theory does not tell us that chairs do not exist, but rather that they, and all other things, are composed only of quantum dots.

The notion of ontological reduction obscures this point. The idea of ontological reduction is that the entities postulated by one theory can be reduced to those postulated by another theory, when the first is explained in terms of the second. For example, heat can be explained in terms of the kinetic energy of molecules and this means that heat has been reduced to molecular movement.

This is a confusing way of explaining scientific explanation, because reduction is not a question of reducing one set of entities to another. As we saw in the previous chapter, reduction is a relation between sets of statements, and not entities. It is a semantic relation. In other words, rather than affirming 'Heat can be reduced to molecular motion,' we should say that statements about heat can be reduced to statements about molecular motion.

The answer to our original problem is as follows. A chair is composed of quantum dots. Is it more than those dots? The answer 'no' seems to miss something out, because for a collection of quantum dots to be a chair, they have to be incredibly well organized. But the answer 'yes' is not correct either, because there is no additional thing involved. The chair is the quantum dots in a special form, or organization. But the form (or organization) is not an additional constituent of the chair. It is not a thing in addition to the atoms.

Following Aristotle, we can distinguish form and matter. Matter is the dots; form is the way in which they are organized. An object is matter in a particular form. However, (and this is the key) form cannot be regarded as an additional matter or constituent, because then it would itself require a form, and so on to infinity.

Conclusion

To counter-act the apparently cold portrait of the universe given by physical sciences, we do not need to postulate the existence of ghosts, souls, spirits, meanings, or values, even if some of these things exist. We only need to be able to truly describe material things in a soulful, spiritual, meaningful or evaluative way. Neither do we have to suppose that such more interesting descriptions have to be reducible to ones in terms of quantum dots.

Appendix: Calculation

A) TIME
Assume that the universe is 20 billion years old.
Assume that the smallest time period (Tbit) is 3×10^{-36} seconds.

1. $T = 2 \times 10^{10}$ years
2. 1 year $= 3 \times 10^{7}$ seconds
3. 1 sec $= 1/3 \times 10^{36}$ Tbits
4. Thus, $T = 2 \times 10^{53}$ Tbits

In other words, the universe has existed for 20 to the power of 53 time bits.

B) SPACE
Assume that the radius of the Universe (R) is 20 billion light-years (LYS). A light year is the distance that light travels in a year.
Assume that the smallest space (Sbit) is 10^{-35} meters.

1. $R = 2 \times 10^{10}$ LYS
2. $1 LY = 10^{16}$ m
3. 1 m $= 10^{35}$ Sbits
4. $R = 2 \times 10^{61}$ Sbits
5. $V = 4/3 \, \Pi R^{3} = 4.2 \, R^{3}$
6. $V = 4.2(2 \times 10^{61})^{3}$ Sbits^3
7. Thus, $V = 33.6 \times 10^{226,981}$ Sbits^3

In other words, the universe has a volume of 33 to the power of 226,981 space bits cubed.

9

Morality without Authorities

It is a dark night; there is a murder. The murderer had no special reason for killing his victim, except dislike. On the basis of this information, would this count as a morally wrong action? Nearly everyone will agree that it was. This leaves us with a problem: What makes an action morally wrong? The question is important, because if we don't know what makes an action morally right or wrong, we cannot hope to find answers to vexing ethical issues, such as euthanasia, or genetic experiments on embryos.

What makes an action morally wrong? Here are some answers that typically emerge in discussion:

1. Each person has his or her own opinion; each person must decide for him or herself what is right and wrong. Therefore, action X is morally wrong if and only if X is in disagreement with the values accepted by the appropriate person. This view is subjectivism.

2. Each society must decide for itself, because what is wrong in one culture might not be in another. Consequently, action X is morally wrong if and only if X is in disagreement with the values accepted by the appropriate society. This theory is called cultural relativism.

3. The essence of morality is constituted by the commandments of God. Action X is wrong if and only if it disagrees with the commands of God. This is the Divine command theory.

4. People have inherent natural rights, which may or may not be enshrined in the law as legal rights. According to this theory, an action X is wrong if and only if it violates someone's natural moral rights. This definition is often called moral rights theory.

As they stand, these theories are incompatible. Although they often agree as to what actions are wrong, sometimes they do not, and therefore, they are incompatible. Moreover, they give conflicting *definitions* of what is to count as a morally right or wrong action. Any one of these definitions automatically rules out the others because it states necessary and sufficient conditions for an action being morally right or wrong (with the words 'if and only if'). The fact that they are incompatible implies that if a person thinks that one of the theories is correct, they must also think that the other three are mistaken.

To understand ethics, we must examine these theories in turn, looking at the arguments and considerations in favor and against each. However, let me be straightforward from the outset and declare that I shall argue that none of these views is plausible. I shall contend that they all are mistaken. Furthermore, I shall argue that the first three positions suffer from the same defect: they assume an authoritarian view of morality. However, later, I shall expand our list, to include better theories.

1) Subjectivism

The first view is called subjectivism. The crucial point to note about it is that it denies that there are 'objective' answers to questions about what is right and wrong. There are no true or false answers to moral questions. (Exactly what this term 'objective' means, I shall come to later).

Apparently in favor of this view, there is the argument that everybody has their own opinion and has to decide for themselves concerning what is morally right and wrong. Otherwise, someone would be deciding for the individual. Furthermore, people have different moral opinions; what is right for me might be wrong for you and, therefore, there is no universal morality. In addition, an absolute morality is inflexible; it does not take into consideration individual circumstances.

The Replies

The last paragraph contained a lot of different points, all mixed together. Let us evaluate them one by one.

1. Each Person Has His or Her Own Opinion:
When we claim that each individual has his or her own moral values or opinions, what does this mean? What is it to have an opinion or accept a moral value? Consider the following steps:

    a)   I accept killing as wrong or, in my opinion, killing is wrong.
    b)   I believe that it is wrong to kill.
    b)   I believe that 'it is wrong to kill' is true.

According to the step from a) to b), accepting a value or having an opinion implies believing something. The sentence 'It is part of my morals not to kill' implies that I believe that it is wrong to kill. But, according to the step from b) to c), the statement 'I believe that p' is equivalent to 'I believe that 'p' is true,' which is also equivalent to 'I believe that 'not p' is false.' In other words, the concepts of belief, true and false are like Siamese triplets; they cannot be separated. This is because it is the essence of beliefs that they can be true or false. Calling them mere opinions cannot sever this link. Any opinion could be false. Therefore, a subjectivist cannot succeed in protecting him or herself from being mistaken by saying 'it is merely my opinion.' Opinions are either true or false.

The phrase 'in my opinion' can be put in front of everything you affirm. For example, to the statement 'I have a nose,' you could add the phrase 'in my opinion.' Everything one affirms is an expression of one's opinion, unless one is lying. Consequently, we cannot employ that phrase to protect what we affirm from being false. Even if we use that phrase, what we say could still be false. Opinions, like beliefs, aim at being true and they can fail; they can be false.

2. People Have Different Opinions:
The fact that there are diverse views about what is morally wrong is supposed to imply that there are no true or false moral judgments. However this argument is not valid because it lacks a premise:

Argument 1:

    a.   <u>There is disagreement about what is right or wrong</u>
    c.   Therefore, there is no objective right and wrong.

For the argument to be valid, the following missing premise must be added:

b.   There is objectivity only if there is agreement.

The problem is that this required premise is false. Unanimity is not a requirement of objectivity or for an assertion to be true or false. Probably, there is never total agreement regarding any statement. For example, there are some people who think that the earth is flat, but that does not mean that there is no objective true or false statement concerning the shape of the planet. Consider Einstein's claim that nothing can travel faster than light. It is either true or false. But whether it is true or false is independent of what people think. Disagreement does not make this merely a matter of subjective opinion.

3. There Are No Universal Moral Rules:
If this means that there are no universally accepted rules, then this is true, but the idea is once again that there exists disagreement. However, as we have already seen in argument one, this is no evidence for subjectivity. The extent of disagreement is irrelevant to the issue.

4. What is Wrong For Me Might Be Right For You:
The crucial expression here is 'for me.' It is ambiguous or has two meanings. First, it can mean 'according to me,' but that is another way of saying 'in my opinion,' which is a point that we have already considered. Adding the phrases 'in my opinion' and 'for me' to a statement does not prevent it from being false, if it is so.

Second, the expression 'for me' has a perfectly normal objective use. For example, when a diabetic claims: 'sugar is bad for me,' he or she is affirming that objectively sugar has bad effects on him or her. Sugar might not have such effects on another person, but this is not at all the same as claiming that, in my opinion, or according to me, sugar is bad. In other words, 'according to me, sugar is bad' is quite different from 'sugar is bad for me.' Thus, we can draw no support for subjectivism from these considerations.

5. Morality is Not Absolute:
Once there was a man who refused to walk because he had learned that the earth does not stand still and is not supported by anything in space. He complained, 'How can I be expected to walk on ground that is unsupported and, worse, is always moving?' When he saw another person walking, he was astounded and explained his worries. The other person frowned and replied: 'You want absolute

foundations. Your mistake is to think that anything less is the same as a free-fall.'

It is a similar mistake to think that only the absolute will suffice and that the only alternative to the absolute is subjectivity. The opposite of 'absolute' is 'relative,' and the opposite of 'objective' is 'subjective.' In other words, the absolute/ relative contrast is distinct from the objective/subjective distinction. Consequently, moral statements can be objective without being absolute. They can be objective, but also relative to the circumstances.

'Morality is absolute' affirms that what is right or wrong does not depend on any other factors. This is a false claim, because what is morally wrong can depend on the context or the situation. However, denying that moral statements are absolute does not mean that they are subjective. Subjectivism and absolutism can both be mistaken.

This is a point of importance because many philosophers have argued that the rejection of absolute values means that we must chose for ourselves what is right and wrong. The death of absolute values means we must embrace subjectivism. We find this position in Nietzche and Existentialism. But this presupposes that absolute and subjective are opposites. It ignores the possibility of moral claims being both objective and non-absolute. We can reject both an absolute and a subjective conception of morality.

What does 'objective' mean? In this case, it has a minimal meaning, namely that value judgments can be true or false. It denies the old adage that thinking makes it so. It implies that value judgments can be true or false independently of what the person making the judgment thinks or decides about their truth or falsity. However, please beware: in other areas of thought, and in other chapters of this book, the term 'objective' has other uses. For example, in science, 'being objective' means being impartial. In the philosophy of psychology, it means without relation to the subject. In metaphysics, it means from no point of view, or even from an absolute point of view. I am not asserting that moral statements are objective in these other senses.

The objectivity of value judgments is equivalent to the idea that we can make mistaken judgments. When subjectivists claim that moral judgments are subjective, this is what they deny. They negate the possibility of error. They deny that value judgments are properly judgments at all, because they are refusing to use the categories 'true' and 'false' in relation to them. In summary,

- Value judgments are objective, not subjective, because what is valuable or morally right does not depend on our beliefs about it. Believing that it is right does not make it so. We can be mistaken.

- Value judgments are relative, not absolute, because what is good or valuable does depend on contextual factors.

6. No one Can Impose His or Her Decision On Me:

This expresses the fear is that someone will try to control you, to tell you what to do in the name of morality. Since we *should* control our own lives, the fear directs us to reject objectivity. However, consider the claim that it would be *wrong* to force-feed morality, the proposition that people *ought* to control their own lives, and the statement that others *should* not tell me what to do. If all of these statements pretend to be true, then they actually presuppose the objectivity of value judgments. Consequently, they cannot be used in the argument against value judgments being true or false. In summary, the fear is legitimate, but it does not legitimize the conclusion that value judgments are subjective. It does not mean that value judgments cannot be true or false.

One can accept that value judgments can be true or false, and still reject sermonizing, stone-throwing and the authoritarian use of morality to control people. Why? Because objectivity means that value judgments are true or false, but the fear - of sermons, stones and authorities- concerns control. Objective value judgments do not imply control. They do not have to be enforced or imposed. It is a bad idea to water the electric socket, but that does not mean that anyone is going to stop you.

We should distinguish moral statements from their execution or enforcement by, for example, the state or unofficial policemen. The moral statement 'You should not hurt your friend' does not imply that someone is going to, or even should, stop you from doing so. Nor does it imply that anyone would be right to criticize you, if you do so. One issue is whether the statement is true; another is whether anyone should enforce it. Following on from this, we can separate two questions:

- In circumstances C, would an abortion be right?
- Should the law allow or forbid abortion in circumstances C?

We might have very different answers to these two questions. For example, abortion could be wrong in C, but yet, the law should not forbid it, but should allow people to act freely. Moral statements do not imply their enforcement.

These points are obliterated when we use authoritarian words to describe what we ought to do, for example, expressions such as 'forbidden,' 'permitted,' and 'what morality orders or tells us to do.' Such expressions suggest that there is an authority that imposes on us.

Although the practice of morality in our society may be authoritarian, the objectivity of moral statements does not mean it should be so.

Subjectivism: the Analysis

Someone in favor of subjectivism might ask: 'Who decides what is right and wrong?' He or she might have asked this at the end of a frustratingly inconclusive discussion about some worrying moral issue. My reply is that the question has a built-in false assumption. It assumes that this is a matter to be decided by some authority in a way that is analogous to a courtroom, with a judge deciding what is right or wrong. The question 'Who decides what is right and wrong?' assumes an authoritarian view of values. The question 'Who is the judge?' arises only if the courtroom picture is correct. If the picture is mistaken, then the original question should not be answered. Instead of 'Who?' we can ask 'What?' (i.e. What are the relevant criteria?)

Those who accept the picture of the courtroom, have to find an answer to the difficult question, 'Who decides?' Some people assert that the answer is God; others claim that it is the community or society; and others, despairing that anyone could have such authority over them, assert: 'It is me. I am the authority, for I am the only judge of what is right or wrong for me.' Subjectivism begins with the acceptance of an authority-based view of values.

The courtroom image is mistaken for two reasons. First, we cannot define right and wrong in terms of the decision of any judge or authority because, if we were to, then it would be impossible to assess the decisions of the judge as good or bad. If a judge decides what is right or wrong, then it would be impossible to say that the judge has decided correctly or erroneously. This is because there would be no independent standards to appeal to, only the decisions of the judge. The argument against defining morality in terms of the decisions of an authority or a judge is as follows:

Argument 2:

1. If morally wrong were to be defined in terms of the decision of an authority, then it would be logically impossible to assess the decisions of the authority as right or wrong.
2. It is logically possible to assess the decisions of an authority as right or wrong.
3. Therefore, morally wrong cannot be defined in terms of the decision of an authority.

This argument has the form: if p then q, and not-q; therefore not-p. It applies to any attempt to define right or wrong in terms of the decisions of an authority - whether the authority is a rational impartial observer, a culture, a community, or the individual, or God. Even the thought that God cannot be mistaken requires the idea that objectively He is right and that thought implies objectivity.

There is a second reason why the courtroom image is mistaken. The eminent rebel physicist declares: 'I have decided that Einstein's theory of Special Relativity is correct after all.' This does not mean that he made it correct by his decision. Rather it means that he has come to believe that it is correct. Analogously, the medical ethics panel declares: 'We have decided that, in some cases, euthanasia is right.' This does not mean that they have made it right by their decision, but that they have come to believe that it is. Similarly, the statement 'We must decide for ourselves' means that we should form our own beliefs, even at the risk of their being false.

However, we should note a weakness in argument 2, namely that a stubborn subjectivist might deny premise 2, arguing that it is indeed impossible to judge the decisions of the authority as right or wrong. This is a point we shall address later.

2) Cultural Relativism

The cultural relativist says that what is right or wrong depends on the values accepted or rejected by a culture or society. Cultural relativism does *not* say that what is thought to be wrong in one society might be believed to be right in another. This is a true and innocuous statement. However, it is sometimes a basis for arguing in favor of cultural relativism. Another argument apparently in its favor is that cultural relativism is more tolerant of other cultures and societies than other views and that, therefore, we should accept it.

Analysis

We can simplify the discussion by pointing out the similarities between cultural relativism and subjectivism. We could call it cultural subjectivism. Like individual subjectivism, cultural relativism makes what is wrong dependent on the values accepted by someone, but, in this case, not the individual, but the group. This means that the position rejects the objectivity of moral claims, just as subjectivism does. As we have seen, objectivity requires the principle that believing or accepting P does not make P true. The objectivity of moral statements implies

108

that they are true or false independently of what any group of people think, wish, or accept about their truth or falsity.

The outcome of the similarity between the two views is that argument two also shows cultural relativism to be false.

Argument 2:

1. If morally wrong were to be defined in terms of the decision of an authority, then it would be impossible to assess the decisions of the authority as right or wrong.
2. It is always possible to assess the decisions of an authority as right or wrong.
3. Therefore, morally wrong cannot be defined in terms of the decision of an authority.

For the sake of clarity, it might help to substitute the term 'the decisions of' with the expression 'what is accepted by' in the above argument. In this case, the defining authority is held to be a culture.

The crucial, and contentious, premise is the second, namely that it is logically possible to evaluate what is accepted by the authority, i.e. the culture or society. This is true because any judge or authority can be right or wrong in what they accept. For example, a society might accept racial discrimination, the killing and torture of minority groups, and slavery. These things are morally wrong, even if they are accepted by a society and, hence, the second premise is justified.

In objection to this argument, it might be asked: 'Who are we to judge another culture in this way?' This question strikes the heart of the issue. Of course, our judgments of another society might be mistaken. But, that is exactly the point, because it implies that value judgments are objective, after all. They can be mistaken.

Returning to the question 'Who are we to judge another culture in this way?', what is important is not *who* says, but rather the content of *what* is said, and whether it is true or false. This is why the question should not be 'Who has the authority to pass moral judgments?' but rather 'What are the relevant criteria?' We should not ask 'Who decides?' but rather 'What are the relevant criteria?'

Replies

Let us turn to the arguments in favor of cultural relativism.

1. What is Wrong in One Society Might Be Right in Another:

This statement has two meanings. First, as we saw with argument 1, the fact that there are differences between societies is not enough to imply that there are no true and false moral claims. Disagreement does not imply subjectivism, or that the truth of moral claims depends on what is accepted. We do not have to search for a universally accepted moral code, because what is true does not depend on what is believed. Moreover, what is accepted in one society might not be in another. But 'accepted' means 'believed to be true,' and that implies objectivity.

In the second sense, the statement may be perfectly true. It may be objectively true that, in one society, X is wrong and that, in another, X is not morally wrong. However, this would be so because the relevant conditions in the two societies are different, and not merely because in one society it is believed that X is wrong and in another not. For example, different cultures have different customs. Imagine a society in which eating the dead is a way to show them respect. This might strike us as a revolting practice, but that is not enough to show that it is morally incorrect in the society in question. To demonstrate that a custom is wrong, one would have to show that it was, for instance, oppressive or harmful. Consequently, such differences of custom do not support cultural relativism. On the contrary, the example shows relativism to be false, because the example involves affirming that the hasty moral judgment 'Eating dead relatives is wrong' is itself false.

What is wrong depends on the circumstances, and in different cultures what is wrong can be different. Therefore, we should not embrace an absolute conception of morality. However, what actions are right or wrong does not depend on what people accept as or believe is right or wrong. For this reason, moral claims are objective and not subjective and cultural relativism is mistaken. Moral judgements can be false: they are objective, but not absolute.

2. Cultural Relativism is Tolerant of Other Cultures:

The idea is that the acceptance of cultural subjectivism would promote greater tolerance between cultures. This, however, cannot be an argument in favor of cultural subjectivism because the point is that we *ought* to be tolerant of other cultures, and this moral 'ought' statement is claimed to be true. Therefore, it implies objectivity.

Even if the acceptance of cultural relativism would promote tolerance, this does not mean it is a true or adequate moral theory. On the contrary, the implicit assumption that intolerance is *bad* undermines the theory, because it appeals to the objective statement 'Intolerance is wrong.' In any case, perhaps, we should not always be tolerant of other cultures. For instance, the world community was tolerant of the apartheid system in South Africa or of slavery for too long.

3) Divine Command Theory

This theory claims that what is wrong is defined by the will of God. This too is an authority-based definition of morality, similar to both subjectivism and cultural relativism. It tries to answer the question 'Who decides what is right or wrong?' Earlier we argued that this question was based on the false assumption that the decisions of some authority define what is right and wrong. To show that this assumption is false, we presented argument 2.

Argument 2 also applies to the Divine Command theory, because the theory is authority-based. We can see this point by considering the following. Suppose we claim that God always makes morally correct choices. This is an evaluation of God's decisions, which implies that 'morally right' is not to be defined in terms of what God wills. It implies that there are moral standards independent of His will.

The same point can be put in form of a famous dichotomy. Does God have a reason for forbidding murder? Suppose that the answer is 'No.' In which case, God's will is arbitrary and He may as well have commanded us to murder each other. On the other hand, suppose that the answer is 'Yes.' In which case, God forbids murder because of those reasons. But, then, it is those reasons that make murder wrong, independently of what God forbids, and this means that the Divine Command theory is mistaken. In other words, there are moral reasons against murder which God perceives perfectly and which His orders reflect perfectly. However, if there are such reasons, then it is these that make murder wrong, and not God's will.

4) Moral Rights

The constitution of a country defines some of the legal rights of its citizens. Others are defined by the courts and by statute. 'What legal rights do we have?' is an empirical issue defined by what the law actually says. However, these legal rights fixed by the law may be supposed to reflect accurately the moral or natural rights that people have independently of the law. For example, people had a moral right to life before any constitution or law was framed. The need for such moral rights is also shown by the fact that the constitution or the law may poorly reflect such rights. For instance, the constitution of the USA famously does not mention any legal right to privacy. Yet the Supreme Court accepted such a right in certain historic legal decisions, apparently because there is such a moral right even before the law recognized it. The theory of moral rights claims that a morally wrong action should be defined in terms of the violation of such rights.

We can begin to discern the problems with this theory by examining the question: 'What is it to have a moral right?' Consider the assertion 'I have a handkerchief.' I can show you the handkerchief and describe its location and size. But this does not apply to moral rights. Consider the claim that I have a legal right. To explain what I mean by this, I can show you the relevant sections of the law that specify the legal right. How can I show you my moral rights?

One might think that moral rights are non-material objects. However, remember our discussion of non-material objects in the case of dualism (see Chapter 6). How does postulating the existence of a non-material thing explain? It does not and to see why consider the following case. Someone threatens your life and the only way to prevent your own murder is for you to kill your would-be assassin. Did the person you killed have a right to life, which you violated? If so, then your action was not justified. Usually, concerning such cases, right theorists claim that the person lost his or her right to life by threatening yours. But lost it, where? How do you lose a right, and how can you regain it? The postulation of a non-material object called a right does not answer such queries.

These puzzling questions put pressure on the notion of having a moral right. However, they do not yet constitute an argument against the notion. The relevant argument is as follows. The claim that I have a right to life means only that other people have an obligation not to kill me without sufficient justification. My rights are other people's obligations and vice versa. But, an obligation appears to be a non-material thing like a right and, so, what does it mean to assert that people have an obligation not to kill? It means that morally they ought not to kill. We have come full circle. The argument against moral rights theory is that, the notion of a moral right presupposes the idea of moral 'ought' statements. It assumes what it is supposed to explain. In other words, we cannot define morality in terms of rights, because we have to elucidate rights in terms of moral 'ought' claims. This does not exclude the possibility that the idea of rights might have some other important role to play in a moral theory.

Reworking the List

I have argued tentatively that the theories represented by 1 to 4 on our original list are all false. They do not explain adequately what is to assert that it is morally wrong to murder. I have argued that in the case of subjectivism, cultural relativism and the Divine Command theory, the reason why they fail is essentially the same: they seek to define 'morally wrong' in terms of the decision of some authority. They endeavor to answer the mistaken question: 'Who decides what is right and wrong?' Now, let us add three new theories to our original list.

5) Morality arises because of a type of social contract between individuals. An action X is morally wrong if and only if it disagrees with the principles that would be part of such a contract. This is called social contract theory.

6) An action is morally right if and only if it causes more general happiness or utility than the alternative actions in the circumstances. This is utilitarianism.

7) As rational beings, persons have free will or autonomy. The essence of morality is that we should try to treat persons as autonomous beings and never merely as means. An action X is morally wrong if and only if the person who performs X does so with the intention of treating another merely as a means. This is Kantian theory.

5) Social Contract Theory

Historically, humans have not, in fact, made a social contract. But we can try to explain the content of morality on the basis of a hypothetical contract, one that it would be rational for people to have made. For instance, imagine that we are gathered together before birth, not knowing in what conditions we will be born. You do not know if you will be a poor or rich person, a man or woman, with ill or good health and so on. Under these conditions, what kind of principles would it be rational for you to agree to as the basis of the society in which you will live? (Rawls, 1971). Such a social contract would include principles prohibiting harm and promoting justice and, according to a social contract theory of morality, a morally wrong action is one that violates such principles.

Social contract theory has serious problems. The most obvious of these is that it excludes moral obligations to other species. Suppose that it would morally wrong to torture a gorilla. This cannot be explained in terms of any hypothetical contract, because such an agreement does not include gorillas. It can be explained, for instance, in terms of the pain and harm done to the gorilla. But, if we have to explain why it is wrong to hurt a gorilla in such terms, then it seems that we should explain it in those same terms for a human, without the need for a social contract.

Second, it is difficult to see how the theory can explain our obligations to future generations. Future generations could not enter into even a hypothetical social contract with us for mutual benefit. They cannot give us benefits. Yet we do have obligations to future generations. We should not pollute the earth to such an extent that it would kill or seriously harm people in the future. Again, it seems that one must explain why we ought not to do so directly in terms of the harm caused to them, without the need for a social contract.

There is a further problem. The theory attempts to explain what is morally wrong by appealing to the decisions which people would hypothetically make. This means that it is an authority-based definition, and that, in this case, the authority is the group that hypothetically enters into a contract. Given that this is correct, then argument 2 shows the theory to be mistaken. Yet again, while these arguments are perhaps not decisive, we have a reason for deleting this theory from our provisional list.

6) Utilitarian Theory

According to utilitarianism, the moral rightness of an action should be defined in terms of the harm or benefit it causes. The whole point of morality is to promote practices and actions that make us better off. Therefore, wrong actions are those that cause more harm or less benefit than their alternatives. An action is morally right if and only if it causes more happiness impartially considered than its alternatives. This theory has three salient features:

a) Traditionally, it considers happiness to be the only non-instrumental value and, therefore, that all other values, such as justice, honesty, and liberty, are only instrumentally good; they are valuable only in so far as they cause happiness or prevent unhappiness. How should happiness be defined? Traditional utilitarian theorists, such as the British philosophers Jeremy Bentham (1748-1832) and John Stuart Mill (1806-73) define happiness in terms of pleasure and the absence of pain. Contemporary utilitarians have defined happiness in terms of preferences and desires. This is a debate for another time.

b) Utilitarianism is a consequentialist theory; the moral value of an action depends only on how far its effects or consequences are good or bad. Therefore, the intention that causes an action does not have direct moral worth. It may have indirect value, however, because an agent who acts out of malice is more likely to cause harm to others later than one who does not.

c) The happiness in question must be impartial. It is not just the agent's own happiness that matters, nor just that of his friends or countrymen. To judge the moral value of an action is to judge the effect that it has on general happiness, impartially considered.

7) Kantian Theory

In Kant's view, moral actions have an intrinsic value. They are valuable, not because their effects, but according to the intention which willed the action. According to Kant's theory, the basis of morality is the autonomy of persons. Each person has an autonomous or free will, and morality requires that we respect this. For instance, it requires that we do not use other people merely as means, but that we should treat persons as valuable in themselves. An action is morally right if and only if the intention from which the action was performed accords with the autonomy of persons.

According to Kantian theory, the rightness or wrongness of an action depends on our will, rather than on its results. What matters morally is that we will in accord with the moral principle, which Kant calls the categorical imperative.

Conclusion

Of the seven moral theories we have examined, only two have survived this initial investigation. The five others have serious weaknesses and, although we have not ruled out the possibility that they might be reformulated so as to overcome these weaknesses, we have seen that their problems are sufficiently serious to discount them in this introductory study. The two that have survived (the utilitarian and Kantian theories) are in conflict. In the next chapter, we shall critically examine these two theories, and the reasons why they conflict, and how it might be resolved.

In this chapter, we have seen that, provisionally, three (and possibly four) theories fail because they try to define what is right and wrong in terms of the decisions of some authority. Morality cannot be based on the decisions of an authority, because it is always in principle possible to assess such decisions of an authority as good or bad.

Appendix 1: Facts and Opinions

To understand things, we often use dichotomies, such as social versus natural, and male and female. A dichotomy has two features: first, it presents us with only two alternatives and, second, the two options are exclusive; nothing can be both.

One of the forces pushing us to subjectivism is the dichotomy between facts and opinions, according to which whatever is not a fact has to be merely an opinion. This dichotomy leads us to depreciate anything that is not a proven scientific fact by assigning it automatically to the category, 'opinion.' Anything which is not science is a merely a matter of opinion, and this means that, with regard to it, there are no true or false answers.

I shall argue that the fact/opinion dichotomy is misleading in two ways. First, the dichotomy confuses at least three distinctions. We have packed too much into the dichotomy and, once we unpack it, we find that it is not always exclusive. Here are the three distinctions:

a) Facts and beliefs: If people believe that the earth is round, then that is an opinion. This implies that opinions can be true or false. Consequently, a sub-set of what people believe is actually true. We have many true beliefs, even if we cannot always identify them as such. This sub-set of true beliefs can also be called 'facts'. Thus, a true belief, such as '2+2=4,' would occur on both sides of the dichotomy: as both a fact, and a belief or opinion. Thus, the dichotomy is not exclusive.

Consider the following absurd conversation. I ask you: "Is water H2O?" You reply: "Yes it is." I exclaim: "But you are expressing your own opinions. Don't give me your opinions. Give me the facts." My comment is absurd for two reasons. First, whatever you affirm will be an expression of your opinion. Everything you assert and believe, unless you are lying, is an opinion. Second, by offering me an opinion that happens to be true, you are also giving me a fact. Fact and opinion are not exclusive.

b) By 'fact' we sometimes mean a statement for which there is evidence. When there is no supporting evidence, we call a statement 'merely an opinion.' This is a misleading use of terms, because it is beliefs that require evidence, and not facts. Therefore, the distinction is between beliefs that are supported by evidence and those that are not. In any case, if value judgments can have evidence to support them, then they can be both facts and opinions.

116

c) The term 'fact' can be employed to refer to a true empirical claim. In contrast, to call something an opinion is (roughly) to affirm that it is a question of likes and dislikes. For example, I like coffee; you do not. The point of calling these likes 'opinions' is to emphasize that, beyond these tastes, there is no fact of the matter whether coffee is better than tea. In view of this, we would claim that this is merely a matter of opinion. According to the dichotomy, anything that is not a matter of empirical fact must be purely a matter of taste. Shortly, I shall argue that this is also a false dichotomy.

The second way a dichotomy can be mistaken is when it presents one with only two alternatives, when actually there are others. For instance, 'Either I am right or I am an idiot' is a false dichotomy because I could be mistaken without being an idiot. The dichotomy of facts and opinions (as explained in c) above) is a false one because there is a third alternative.

A claim does not have to be either an empirical fact or else merely a matter of taste. One alternative is that it is a priori. As we saw in Chapter 1, mathematics does not consist of empirical statements. The statement '2 + 2 = 4' is not a true empirical generalization; it is an a priori truth. In this sense, 2+2=4 is not an empirical fact, but that does not mean that it is a matter of taste. You could say it is a truth of reason. The dichotomy leaves out this last option. Concerning morality, the dichotomy of fact and opinion omits the possibility that some moral judgments are a priori truths.

Are moral judgments purely a matter of taste, of likes and dislikes? Consider the following: I hate George and you propose to harm him. I say to you: "I would like you to harm him, but it would be morally wrong to do that. You should not do it." My statement is not a contradiction. However, it would be one, if morality were purely a matter of taste, or of likes and dislikes. If moral judgments were merely an expression of likes and dislikes then, the sentence 'I would like you to do X but X is morally wrong' would not make sense. Therefore, morality is not merely a question of taste.

Of course, we sometimes do confuse moral judgments with those of taste. For example, a person might claim that it is morally wrong to belch at the table. However, such an affirmation would be false because it confuses morality and good manners.

Appendix 2: Verbs, Nouns and Adjectives

Any consideration of values has to be clear with regard to the differences between sentences of the following three forms: 'I value X,' X is a value' and 'X is valuable.' In the first sentence-form 'value' is a verb; in the second, it functions like a noun; and the third employs the adjectival form 'is valuable.' In this appendix, I shall very briefly outline reasons for thinking that, of these three forms, the third is the least misleading.

First and foremost, there is a fundamental difference between, for instance, 'I value friendship' and 'friendship is valuable.' The first sentence tells us a psychological fact about a person, which we could verify with an empirical test. The second is a value claim, as are sentences of the form 'I ought to...' 'We should...' and 'It is good that...' We need to distinguish evaluative claims from psychological ones.

The English language sometimes makes this distinction difficult to manage. Consider the following two points.

a) First, the verb 'to value' indicates certain psychological states, such as wanting, judging, deciding and placing value on and, as such, the verb form is used to make empirical claims about people. Such empirical claims are not evaluative statements, for instance, concerning the quality of life or what actions we should perform. As a consequence of all this, we should beware of employing the verb form 'to value' when we wish to make an evaluative claim.

b) Second, the noun use of 'value,' in sentences such as 'our values are...' and 'friendship is a value,' suggests that values are entities or objects that are constructed and possessed. This form of discourse can seduce us into thinking that values are created and owned. It reifies value. Enough was said against reifying in Chapters 5, 6 and 7 and we do not need to repeat those arguments here.

These two ways of thinking and talking obfuscate the difference between factual and evaluative judgments. If the noun and the verb forms are misleading, then it would be better to think in terms of the adjectival phrase or the predicate 'is valuable.' Of the three forms, this is the primary. This point supports one of the conclusions of Chapter 8, when we tried to endorse the possibility of evaluative descriptions in a world of extensionally characterized dots. It defends the assertion that evaluations are a form of description that can be true or false.

10

Morality without Rules

Should our society legalize capital punishment for certain kinds of murder? Let us define category-A murders as follows: those that are intentionally committed with foresight and malice, and for which the evidence is not merely circumstantial. (There may be other conditions that you wish to include). Should there be capital punishment for such murders? Let us see how a typical discussion might proceed. In favor of capital punishment, there are the following points:

- Capital punishment is an effective deterrent.
- It prevents repeat offences.
- The greater the crime, the greater the punishment deserved; the greatest of all crimes deserves the greatest punishment.
- Capital punishment is a less expensive option than long-term prison sentences; and the prisons are full.
- An eye for an eye: this is the central idea of justice.

The following points might be raised against capital punishment:

- If killing is wrong, so is capital punishment.
- When we take into account the cost of appeals, capital punishment is not a less expensive option.
- Capital punishment is not an effective deterrent because deterrence depends on whether the murderer thinks he or she is likely to be caught.
- Capital punishment is irreversible, and mistakes are made.
- Human life does not have a price; even if capital punishment is cheaper, it is not justified.

Section I: Setting up the Conflict

None of these points constitute an argument. They are more like potential arguments. Also, the list is not complete. Leaving these caveats aside, what should we do with these two lists? How can we be clearer about the issue? One idea is to reorganize the points as follows:

IN FAVOR

BOX 1
a)   The greater the crime, the greater the punishment deserved; the greatest of all crimes deserves the greatest punishment;
b)   An eye for an eye: this is the central idea of justice

BOX 2
c)   Capital punishment is an effective deterrent.
d)   It prevents repeat offences.
e)   Capital punishment is a less expensive option than long-term prison sentences; and the prisons are full.

AGAINST

BOX 3
A)   If killing is wrong, so is capital punishment.
B)   Human life does not have a price; even if capital punishment is cheaper, it is not justified.
C)   It is irreversible and mistakes are made.

BOX 4
D)   Capital punishment is not an effective deterrent because deterrence depends on whether the murderer thinks he or she is likely to be caught.
E)   Once we take into account the cost of appeals, capital punishment is not a less expensive option.

We can simplify the boxes even further as follows:

121

FOR	**AGAINST**
BOX 1: It is just	BOX 2: It is unjust
BOX 3: It is efficient	BOX 4: It is inefficient

Boxes 3 and 4 are similar. They both appeal to utilitarian considerations; they both regard capital punishment merely as a means to an end. The difference between them is only whether it is an efficient means. In this sense, they agree fundamentally on what the issue is.

Compare them to boxes 1 and 2. These two are not concerned with whether capital punishment is an efficient means, but rather whether it is intrinsically just. These are Kantian positions.

Boxes 1 and 2 agree on what the issue is and, in this respect, disagree with boxes 3 and 4. This difference is more important than being in favor or against capital punishment. Box 3 has more in common with 4 than 1 and, box 1 has more in common with 2 than 3. Or, in other words, the horizontal line marks a more important distinction than the division between for and against, because this horizontal line indicates what the debate is about. The fundamental discussion should not be between those persons who are in favor and those who are against capital punishment, but rather between the views which are above and those below the horizontal line.

To understand this point, compare box 1 and 3. The term 'punishment' has a different sense for each of the two boxes. Consider box 3. Suppose you have a young child who is about put his hand on a hot stove. You punish him. But you do not punish him in the sense of box 1. You do not exclaim: 'You naughty boy; you deserve this punishment.' Rather, the punishment is merely a means to prevent him from doing it again. This adopts a box 3 and 4 view of punishment, according to which punishment is merely valuable as a means. For box 1, it is intrinsically valuable and deserved. In this way, the term 'punishment' has different senses for box 1 and 3.

This last point has surprising consequences. It means that, as they stand, boxes 1 and 3 are incompatible, because, whereas 1 says that capital punishment is intrinsically deserved, 3 says that it is merely a means. Suppose, it could be scientifically demonstrated that capital

122

punishment actually increases the murder rate. In such a case, a person supporting box 3 ought to switch to box 4, but the proponent of box 1 should not. Or, suppose that it could be shown scientifically that capital punishment dramatically decreases the murder rate, then a person in box 4 ought to switch to box 3, but those in box 2 should not.

Furthermore, one cannot try to support box 1 with considerations from box 3. We could not justify the claim that wrong actions intrinsically deserve punishment by claiming that this would promote a more peaceful society. This would be equivalent to claiming that X is intrinsically valuable because it is instrumentally valuable.

We began with a mess: a jumble of points. We have put order into this confusion and, as a result, we have revealed the deeper nature of the conflict, one that is embodied in our very legal system: Is our legal system merely a means or is it concerned with justice? This process of clarification begins to show what the real issues are.

This extended example also shows how a little analysis can separate and clarify the utilitarian and Kantian elements in a moral conflict. The same kind of analysis can be extended to other moral conflicts, such as reverse discrimination or affirmative action policies. Are such policies intrinsically just? Those of a Kantian tendency would argue that this is the issue we should be focused on. The utilitarian would argue that, instead, we should be concentrating on whether such policies are efficient means to certain goals. Once again, they contest the nature of the issue.

Everyday morality contains these two components: the Kantian and the utilitarian. But they conflict. Before we address how the clash might be resolved, let us examine its nature. To recap, utilitarian theory says that an action is morally right insofar as it has the result of causes happiness or general utility more than the alternative actions available in the context. The classical utilitarian text is J.S. Mill's *Utilitarianism*. On the other hand, the Kantian theory claims that an action is morally right if the will of the agent was moved by the Categorical Imperative. Kant asserts that the intentions behind our actions should accord with this fundamental moral principle, irrespective of the results. In one of its forms, this principle claims that we should never treat a person as a mere object, as a mere means to some further ends. We should respect persons as such, as free autonomous beings. The classical exposition of this view is Kant's *Groundwork of the Metaphysics of Morals*.

To summarize the most pertinent differences between the two theories:

1. The utilitarian view is consequentialist, which means that only the results or consequences of our actions matter morally. It does not matter directly how those effects are produced. On the other hand, in the Kantian-type theory what matters morally is the will that caused the action, and the results of the action do not.
2. The utilitarian theory holds that the only thing of intrinsic value is welfare or happiness. There are other values, such as autonomy and retributive and distributive justice, but these are valuable only in so far as they lead to more happiness. They are only instrumentally valuable. On the other hand, the Kantian theory holds that autonomy and retributive justice are intrinsic values. Happiness should be deserved and our actions should respect the fact that other people are choosers and have a free-will. Justice and autonomy are non-instrumental values.

The two theories overlap to a considerable degree in that they often recommend the same actions. For example, both would claim that we have some obligation to help others. They would also state that, in most circumstances, murder is wrong. Despite this agreement, they disagree radically over what makes an action right or wrong, and therefore, they are incompatible, although, we can try to revise both theories to make them compatible.

Should doctors lie to their patients when it would harm the patient to tell them the truth? The Kantian and utilitarian answers to this question are very different. According to the utilitarian, the main issue is the well-being of the people involved. It might be wrong to lie, if, for example, this became known and the medical profession became discredited as a result. Lying might have harmful side effects. In such a case, lying would be wrong because the overall effect would be detrimental. According to utilitarianism, whether the lie is wrong or not depends on its future effects - whether they are on the whole beneficial or harmful.

For the Kantian, on the other hand, lying does not respect the autonomy of the patient. Therefore, it is wrong independent of its future consequences. Lying would constitute using another person as a means, and this is wrong, even if we are using the person to help him or her.

Let us look at another example. Would it be wrong to break a promise, if by doing so one helps someone else? The utilitarian would answer this question by looking at the likely future effects of breaking the promise. As in the previous example, there are important, negative side effects to consider such as 'Would this encourage others to break their promises?' If so, the useful social institution of promise keeping might be damaged. On the other hand, Kantian theory would not consider such future effects. According to this theory, the reason to keep our promises is not future effects, but rather, the past – namely, the fact that one has promised. It is not a question of weighing future benefits and harms. We saw a similar point in the discussion of punishment. For the utilitarian, the justification of punishment lies in its future beneficial effects. For the Kantian, it lies in the past - the wrong act that deserves the punishment.

Arguments against Utilitarian Theory

A man has been accused of murdering a child. The town is very angry and wants the man to be punished immediately by hanging. The judge, however, suspects that the man may be innocent. Suppose that he is right. Suppose, also that if the hanging does not take place, the town will riot, and in that riot many people will be killed. Should the innocent man be hung? (This example is taken from Rachels, 1999).

The critique is as follows: according to utilitarian theory, the man should be hung but, in fact, that would be a wrong action and, therefore, utilitarianism is mistaken. Other counter-examples can be constructed along similar lines. The general form of the argument can be expressed as follows:

1. In circumstances C, utilitarianism will recommend action A.
2. Action A is morally wrong
3. Therefore, utilitarianism is mistaken

Utilitarians can respond to this argument in two ways. First, they can deny premise 1, arguing that this premise ignores important side effects. Once it becomes known that an innocent man has been hung, the legal system would be damaged, and the resultant harm would be much greater than that of the riot. Furthermore, if the innocent man is hung, then the guilty person goes free, and may commit repeat offenses. Therefore, utilitarianism does not recommend action A.

In reply to this defense, we can amend the example. Suppose that no-one ever finds out that an innocent man was hung, and suppose that the guilty person never repeats his offense. In such a case, the utilitarian would have to claim that action A was right, and yet, A would still be a morally wrong action. So, utilitarianism is false.

The utilitarian can respond to the altered example by denying premise 2. If there are no important side effects, then action A would not be morally wrong. If there were a way to prevent the riot without killing the accused, then that would be better. However, given that this is impossible, it would be better to kill the accused than have many more people die in a riot.

The counter-reply, or the reply to the utilitarian response, involves appealing directly to a Kantian notion of justice. According to this, even if lots of people die in a riot, it is still wrong to punish an innocent person. It is unjust.

Arguments against Kantian Theory

Suppose that it is World War Two. You are a Dutch citizen and there is a Jewish family hiding in your house. The Gestapo come and ask you if there are any Jews living in the house. You can lie, in which case the Gestapo will go away and the family can be saved. On the other hand, if you tell the truth, the family will be taken away to a concentration camp and killed (see Rachels, 1999). The argument against the Kantian theory says that the Kantian must tell the truth, but this would be a morally wrong action and, therefore, Kantian theory is mistaken. We could construct other examples along these lines, and the general form of the argument would be:

1. In circumstances C, Kantian theory will recommend action A.
2. <u>Action A is morally wrong</u>.
3. Therefore, Kantian theory is mistaken.

Notice that this argument has a similar form to the one against utilitarianism, and so do the replies and counter-objections, which you can supply for yourself. What do we learn from this similarity? First, to find a good moral theory, we need to use examples of right and wrong actions to test the theory. Furthermore, we can amend the examples to explore the implications of the theory. However, to use examples in this way, we need to employ ones that are not contentious. Second, we learn that arguments against utilitarianism typically appeal to Kantian notions, and vice versa. This shows that the arguments are not completely decisive. The argument against one theory presupposes the truth of the other. This reveals the conflict between the two theories, but not any conclusive argument in favor of any one of them.

Section II: The Conflict

To appreciate the force of the conflict, let us examine some more examples. The conflict between Kantianism and utilitarianism is a deep moral dilemma, as the following examples shall show. Such a dilemma has at least three features:

First, the answer must matter. Truman had to decide whether to launch an atomic bomb against Japan and he would not have tossed a coin to decide the issue, because it mattered.

Second, in a deep dilemma, the contention cannot arise only through a lack of information. There has to be at least two options to choose between and it must not be the case that one of those options would be obviously better than the other given some particular empirical fact. When the conflict arises only because of our ignorance on some factual point, we can bet (for instance, on which outcome is the most likely). Betting is not a solution for deep moral conflicts, but only for situations in which we lack sufficient empirical information.

Third, a deep moral dilemma requires that there is a solution to be discovered. Without a solution to find, there would be no conflict and no reason to fret. Given that there are two alternative actions A and B to choose between, then there are three possible solutions: either you should do A; or you should do B; or else the two actions are indifferent. Being convinced that there is a solution to a conflict does not imply that you or anyone knows that solution. All it means is that there is something to know or to discover.

The examples that follow constitute deep moral dilemmas because they satisfy the above criteria. The first examples are designed to make the Kant in you sweat, and to appeal to the utilitarian in you. After that, I will give an example against the utilitarian position, which will resuscitate the Kantian viewpoint. These examples do not constitute arguments. They are designed to appeal to different intuitions. They may not work for everyone, but you should understand the point.

Example 1:

Imagine that you are walking in the hills of Bolivia in the year 1947. You come across a small village and in the square, there is a police chief who is about to execute four native Indians. You know that the Indians are not guilty of any crime, and the police chief is planning to kill them out of malice. The police chief sees you and welcomes you as a foreign guest. He says: "In order to celebrate your arrival as a special visitor, I propose to let the four Indians go free, but only if you shoot another Indian. If you refuse my offer, I will go ahead and shot all four as I had planned." Should you agree to this? In this example, you cannot shoot the police chief, nor yourself; nor can you speak to the victims. Should you shoot? (The example is based on Williams, 1973)

A slight majority of people claim that one should not shoot. A large minority claim that one should. According to the utilitarian theory, the latter is the correct answer. After all, you would be saving three lives. Utilitarianism recognizes no difference between your performing the action and the police chief doing so, because, for utilitarianism, what is uniquely important is the results of action, the end state - namely, the fact that in one option only one person dies, and in the other four die. There is no important difference between your killing and your failing to prevent the police chief from doing so.

Those who oppose shooting one to save three will challenge this utilitarian approach by arguing: 'I am not responsible for what the police chief does. I am responsible for my own actions, and it is wrong for me to kill.' In saying this, they are articulating a Kantian point of view, namely that one is not right to use one person to save three.

Example 2:
The following example is directed to those who think it is wrong to kill one person to save three, i.e. to the Kantians. (If you are more utilitarian, then please wait for the third example). To place our Kantian intuitions under pressure and to emphasize the utilitarian element in our conception of morality, I will now alter the first example. Imagine now that you are offered the opportunity to kill one innocent person to save a million lives.

I assume that the majority of people who originally were not willing to shoot one person to save three have now changed their mind. In other words, I assume that you now think that it would not be wrong to kill one person to save a million lives. In which case, your intuitions have changed; they have become utilitarian.

If you persist in thinking that it is wrong to kill one to save so many lives, then I would like to put a couple of points to you.

a) Perhaps, you are thinking that numbers don't count. But we are not talking about numbers; we are talking about people and their lives. Killing is wrong because death is bad, and a million deaths is worse than one. To make this more apparent, consider the second point.

b) I assume that you think that it would be not be wrong for you to kill a person who was going to murder you, if there was no other way to save your own life. In which case, you claim that it is right to kill in self-defense, as long as this is strictly necessary. Given this, I ask you: Why is it right to kill one to save one, when earlier you said it was wrong to kill one to save a million? Imagine that your family and friends are amongst the million. In this situation, I think that you would claim that it is not wrong to kill one person to save many.

My first aim was to convince those readers who originally thought it was wrong to kill one to save three that they should be willing to abandon their Kantian intuitions, and adopt a more utilitarian point of view, when there are considerably more lives at stake. I hope that I have achieved this objective.

Example 3:
I want now to address those readers who would say of the original example, that they should kill one person to save three. I want everyone to feel the pressure! I shall now dispute the utilitarian intuitions, which a moment ago I was trying to uphold. In other words, now I shall support the Kantian intuitions that I have just challenged. The third example is that of involuntary organ donation. (This example is adapted from Harris, 1975).

Imagine that a select group of influential doctors decide to institute a practice of involuntary organ donation. The doctors know each other well and will keep their vow of silence. They make a pact and their idea is as follows. They divide their patients into several groups: category A patients are healthy people who will not be missed, who are known not to have immediate family and friends. If you are a category A patient then, when you visit the doctor with an ear infection, he or she will say: 'In order to study your problem properly, I need to give you a general anesthetic, and put you to sleep.' While you are asleep, the doctor reasons as follows: 'This person has eight pints of fresh blood, a good liver, kidneys and heart, young eyes; and with these organs we could save the lives of at least four poor people who would otherwise die.'

Should we practice involuntary organ donation? I believe that most of my readers would reply: 'Definitely not.' The reasons are essentially Kantian: such a practice infringes autonomy; it is heavily paternalistic, and ignores the rights of persons to decide for themselves about the use of their bodies. But, from the utilitarian point of view, in terms of the results, this third example is the same as the first one: we save four lives by sacrificing one.

The Interim Conclusion:

Morality appears to consist of broadly both Kantian and utilitarian elements. In saying this, I do not mean to endorse the specifics of either position. For example, one may take issue with the utilitarian conceptions of utility maximization and of happiness, and with the Kantian conception of the will. Rather, the point is that the results of our actions do matter, and so do the intentions from which we act. Furthermore, both well-being and autonomy matter too. In both cases, both elements are necessary. Yet, as they stand, the two positions are contradictory. However, it is not good enough just to assert that we need both and leave it at that. If morality comprises both elements, then we need to know when each one of the views is applicable, and according to what criteria. We have to know when and why.

There is a final and important point. We cannot evade these conflicts by appeal to a decision-procedure, at least without some argument to that effect. In normal life, when we decide what to do, we often adopt some kind of decision-procedure, which is a set of guidelines for making decisions. Examples might include the following: 'Calmly consider the options and weigh the probable effects of each' and 'consider what a community of rational communicators would decide.' Such decision-procedures give practical help. However, they do not tell us when decisions are morally right or wrong, because they do not specify the truth-conditions for moral statements. Because moral judgments can be true or false, as students of moral philosophy, we have the task of specifying the criteria that make specific judgments true or false. In other words, we must identify the truth-conditions for moral claims. Giving a decision procedure does not accomplish that. For example, the suggestion that, to solve conflicts, some rational judge should decide presents a decision procedure. However, it does not solve the problem of specifying the truth-conditions for the relevant moral claims. It does not tell us according to what criteria such a judge would decide. It is this task of giving truth-conditions that we need to complete in order to resolve moral conflicts.

Section III: The Nature of the Conflict

The conflict between utilitarianism and Kantian theory has two features. First, traditionally, utilitarianism is a monistic theory. It claims that happiness or well-being is the only non-instrumental value and other values, such as autonomy and justice, are only instrumental. The traditional utilitarian argument in favor of monism is that ethical reasoning requires it. If monism were not true, conflicts of value would not have a solution.

However, monism is false. There is not only one intrinsic value, but many. Candidates apart from happiness include autonomy, deserts, and distributive justice. To see this, imagine two worlds both with the same overall happiness, but in one, the happiness is relatively evenly distributed and, in the other, there are a few people who are very happy and many people who are unhappy. Is there a reason for thinking that the first world is better than the second one? There is. The first world is more just. This implies that justice is an intrinsic value that can compete with happiness.

Let us return to an earlier example. The only way to prevent a violent riot that will result in many deaths is to hang an innocent man. Is there a non-instrumental reason against the hanging? There is. The mere fact that the man is innocent and does not deserve punishment. This implies that desert is another intrinsic value. Each of these examples can generate a debate, but we must move on. Let us tentatively accept the claim that there is more than one intrinsic value. In fact, some contemporary utilitarians accept a plurality of intrinsic values, but they must explain how conflicts between such values can be resolved. How they might do this is beyond the scope of this book.

The second feature of the conflict is that utilitarianism is consequentialist, and Kantian theory is not. The utilitarian asserts and the Kantian denies that, morally speaking, only the results of our actions directly matter. We can see the implications of this difference in the earlier examples. For the utilitarian, there is no intrinsic difference between performing an action oneself and allowing someone else to do it, so long as the results are the same. Consider euthanasia. Are there any differences between passive and active euthanasia for terminally ill patients? In passive euthanasia, the doctors do nothing to kill such a patient; they merely let him or her die by not providing life-support treatment. In active euthanasia, the doctors actively do something to bring about an early death, such as a lethal injection. In the one case, they let the patient die; in the other, they kill him.

However, when the results are the same, does this difference between killing and letting die actually amount to anything of importance? According to the utilitarian, if all other things are equal and the results are the same, then it does not. According to the Kantian, it does because, in the one case, we actually will the death of someone, and in the other, we don't.

The euthanasia example is complex because the results of active and passive euthanasia are not the same. Let us construct an example that better serves to illustrate the real issue. Your wealthy, old uncle is in the bath. He has an electric fire in his bathroom, which is precariously perched on a rickety shelf. You do not like your uncle and stand to inherit millions when he dies. You want the old man dead.

1. In the first case, to make the electric fire fall into the bath, you only have to stamp your foot on the floor. This is what you do, deliberately and knowingly. You kill him.

2. In the second case, to stop the electric fire falling in the bath, you only have to stamp your foot on the floor. Deliberately and knowingly, you don't do it. You let him die.

Is there a moral difference between the two cases? Is the first case worse than the second? If it is, then the Kantian is right to insist that there is an intrinsic difference between doing and letting happen. If it is not, then the utilitarian is right to claim that there is no such difference.

Section IV: Combination

One way to resolve the conflict between the two theories is to try to combine them. Since they are incompatible as they stand, this requires modifying them. There are two principal ways to make such modifications.

1) Rule-utilitarianism

As a diagnosis, one strength of utilitarianism is its claim that the overall aim of morality is to improve our well-being. Its principal defect is that it directly recommends specific actions. Is there a way to keep this strength and reject the defect? Consider promise keeping. It involves doing what you promise to do even when breaking the promise is beneficial. You should keep your promises, even when breaking them would maximize utility. Therefore, promising gives us a non-utilitarian reason for acting.

Nevertheless, the institution of promise keeping itself is immensely beneficial; it forms the backbone of all contracts and business. Without it, we would be much worse off. Consequently, paradoxical though it seems, we have a utilitarian consideration, which gives us non-utilitarian reasons for acting.

Similar points can be made about retributive justice. It is a system that provides non-utilitarian reasons for acting; we should punish the guilty and not the innocent, irrespective of utilitarian calculations. Yet, despite this, the whole system of retributive system can be given a utilitarian justification, because we are better off with such a system than without it. Paradoxically, there are utilitarian reasons for a system that enjoins us sometimes to act in a non-utilitarian way.

According to the rule-utilitarian, none of this is paradoxical. We should distinguish two levels of moral thought and practice:

a) The setting up of moral rules, and
b) The judging of particular acts according to those rules.

The first level is utilitarian, but the second is not. Particular actions should be judged right or wrong according to moral rules, which are not utilitarian, such as 'Do not lie,' and 'Never punish the innocent.' However, at the first level, these non-utilitarian rules themselves should be justified according to utilitarian considerations.

This seems to be a fruitful idea. It preserves the integrity of non-utilitarian reasons for action, but at the same time, recognizes that the overall point of morality is to improve the quality of life. According to this idea, the utilitarian principle should not be applied to individual actions, but rather to a system of rules. These rules determine the criteria that make particular actions right or wrong.

However, traditional act-utilitarians (those who think that the utilitarian principle should be applied directly to actions) argue that the rule-utilitarian position is unsustainable. They do so by arguing that it will end up recommending exactly the same actions as the normal act-utilitarian position. In order to maximize happiness, we will have to keep amending the rules (Smart, 1973). One way around this objection, which we shall not pursue, is to abandon the idea that utilitarianism should seek to maximize well-being or happiness, while retaining a broadly consequentialist framework. In other words, we can affirm that an action can be wrong because of its harmful results, without asserting that happiness must always be maximized.

2) Side Constraints

Some thinkers have argued that morality consists of utilitarianism with Kantian-like constraints. In other words, morality bids us to act so as to increase general happiness, but without infringing the autonomy of others. This is a promising solution, but it also has a problem. For example, in extreme cases, when we can dramatically improve the well-being of lots of people by infringing someone's autonomy in a minor way, then arguably we should do so. In other words, it can be argued that autonomy rights have limits too. But, what limits? What makes a case extreme? How dramatic does the improvement in well-being have to be? To solve practical conflicts, we need answers to these questions, which the theory does not provide.

Section V: Morality without Rules

We have examined the conflict between the utilitarian and Kantian elements of morality and some ways of resolving this conflict. Now I want to suggest why this problem is so intractable. It is that in specifying the criteria for what we ought to do, we have assumed that this must consist in moral rules that determine what we ought to do and why. In this section, I shall argue that no such moral rules are possible.

5.1 Conclusive Reasons

A conclusive reason for action is one that, in the circumstances, is not overridden by another reason. A person has a conclusive reason to do action A if there is no other action in the circumstances for which the person would have a better reason, all things considered. The definition shows us that conclusive-reason claims are very strong. They represent the overall best action in the situation. This means that conclusive reasons for action are essentially circumstantial. It is only in a particular situation that one can truly say that someone has a conclusive reason to act or not act in a specific way. Morality cannot be based on general rules that give conclusive reasons for action. General rules that state conclusive reasons for action, such as 'Never lie,' are not correct. They are subject to exceptions, which is another way of saying that they are false.

We should not hope to overcome this problem by building the exceptions into the rules, by constructing rules of the following kind: 'Do not kill, except when....' The problem is that the final clause cannot be completed. Until it is completed, the whole statement is false. If one accepted the statement 'I ought not kill except in the following circumstances...' and, if there were a situation in which it was right to kill that was left off the list, then the original statement would be false. In other words, the list has to be complete, and this requirement is impossible to satisfy. Rules have to be rigid.

The final clause specifying the exceptions cannot be completed because the list must be open-ended. There is an indefinite number of circumstances in which one could have an overriding reason to kill to someone. For every situation in which one thinks killing would be permissible, there are others that one has not even conceived of.

We can draw the following important conclusion: it is possible for a conclusive-reason statement to be true only in specific circumstances. This shows that moral understanding cannot be captured with general, conclusive-reason rules that will cover all circumstances, because the content of morality is essentially open-textured.

Neither can we use rules that are tautological, because these do not provide any guidance. For example, 'Do not kill unless there are overriding reasons to do so' says the same as 'Do what you ought to do.' Both are tautological and give no guidance.

5.2 Non conclusive Reasons

We can frame true general moral rules in terms of non-conclusive reasons, such as 'There is a reason not to kill,' or 'There is a reason not to cause pain.' A statement that a person has a reason to do A can be true, even though the person has a better reason to do something else. Reasons can be overridden by other better reasons. Certainly, there is always a reason against killing, even if that reason is not always conclusive. A reason for action can be defeated by a better reason to do something else. There are true general moral rules couched in non-conclusive reason terms, such as 'There is always a reason not to kill.' However, the trouble is that such rules cannot be used to guide action.

Obviously, non-conclusive reasons can conflict: we can have (non-conclusive) reasons to do and not do the same action in any specific situation. For example, I have a non-conclusive reason not to lie, but I also have a reason not to cause suffering. When we ask 'Should I tell the person the awful and terrible truth?' these reasons conflict. On the other hand, conclusive reasons for action do not conflict, simply because they are conclusive. They define the best action in the situation, all things considered.

Consequently, if we tried to frame the content of morality in terms of rules that specify non-conclusive reasons for action, then morality would not tell us what we conclusively ought to do in any particular situation. Although rules of this weaker type can be true in all circumstances, they only provide the first step in practical reasoning. Statements that specify non-conclusive reasons do not make a comparison between the force and importance of those reasons, and are too weak to determine what we should do all things considered.

5.3 Better Reasons

On the one hand, there are conclusive-reason statements (which determine what we should do, but are too strong to be true general rules) and, on the other hand, there are non-conclusive reason statements (which can yield true general rules, but which are too weak to determine what we should do). There is an alternative to these two options, which is to try to frame general rules in terms of comparative reason statements, of the form 'X is a better reason for action than Y.' For example, 'Needs provide stronger reasons for action than desires, all other things being equal.' However, even such statements do not tell us what we should do all things considered in particular situations.

We can conclude that general rules do not determine what we should do. On the one hand, statements that specify conclusive reasons for action are always singular judgments and context specific. On the other hand, general statements or rules that specify non–conclusive reasons for action do not tell us definitively what we conclusively to do in particular circumstances. Rules can guide action without determining it. The content of morality cannot be specified exclusively with rules.

Section IV: Conclusion

This conclusion has important implications for how we should regard practical reasoning and morality. It indicates that we should be wary of defining morality in terms of the right action and practical reasoning in terms of conclusive reasons. This is because general rules cannot legislate for particular circumstances, and conclusive reasons are essentially circumstantial.

The problem is that, in the definition of a conclusive reason, the term 'the best' functions as an expression without any restrictions, and which requires us to take all points of view and consider all the possible criteria. This requires a complete totality with regard to all possible criteria of evaluation. Conclusive rules are too strong and non-conclusive rules too weak to capture the guidance of morality in specific situations. This shows us that moral understanding cannot consist only in knowing fixed rules, because the content of morality is essentially open-textured.

The scope of morality is limited by the impossibility of giving generalized solutions that are not too weak or too strong. In conclusion, it is futile to hope for general moral rules that will determine what we conclusively ought to do in specific circumstances. Rules can guide us but not dictate a particular solution. This does not mean that there is not a solution to moral dilemmas. It only means that there is no solution defined by a rule.

This conclusion opens the way for other attempts to gain a deeper understanding of morality. It opens the possibility, for instance, for virtue-based ethics, which argue that the important question is not 'What actions are right and wrong?' but rather 'What kinds of persons should we be?' or 'What virtues should be encourage and what vices should we discourage in ourselves?'

Appendix: the Naturalistic Fallacy

Suppose that some normative statements are a priori (following the appendix of the previous chapter). Let us suppose further that all a priori statements are analytic. This implies that some moral statements are analytic. But is this a reasonable conclusion?

Let us begin with a simple statement:

1. Pain is bad

There are two objections to the claim that this is an analytic statement. First, pain is not always bad. For example, the pain of an injection need not be bad. But an analytic truth must always be true, and therefore 1 is not an analytic or an a priori truth.

To answer this objection, we need to make two distinctions. First, we should distinguish instrumental and non-instrumental value. Some things are only instrumentally good or bad. They are good or bad only because of their effects (for example, money and the lack of it). This implies that other things are non-instrumentally good or bad: i.e. good or bad because of what they are, not just because of what they lead to (for example, pain and pleasure).

Second, we need to distinguish conclusive and non-conclusive reasons for action. As we have already seen, in a dilemma, two non-conclusive reasons conflict. There is a reason for you both to keep your promise to visit a friend on Saturday afternoon and to visit you grandmother in hospital; you cannot do both. But you have reason to do both and because of this both actions are good. Which of the reasons is stronger? When you have answered that question, you have solved the dilemma. Non-conclusive reasons should be distinguished from conclusive reasons. With these distinctions in mind, we can amend 1 as follows:

2. Pain is non-conclusively and non-instrumentally bad.

Statement 2 does not seem vulnerable to the first objection to 1.

The second objection is that the denial of an analytic truth is a contradiction, and that denying 1 is not a contradiction. However, in reply to this, it seems quite reasonable to hold that to deny 2 would be a contradiction. We can see this by considering the nature of classification. For example, some things are chairs, and others are not. In other words, when we classify things into the two classes, chairs and non-chairs, it is possible to make mistakes. Of course, there might be unclear cases, but that is beside the point. The classification is objective. Now let us ask: 'What is a chair?' A reasonable first definition might be: 'An object made for the purpose of sitting on it.' We cannot explain the concept of a chair without mentioning the human interest we have in chairs, because that is why we classify certain objects as chairs. Therefore, the classification is interest-based. From this, we can conclude that the classification is both objective and interest-based.

Now let us turn to pain. We can make mistakes in classifying pain. A friend falls over; you think he is in terrible agony, but really he is laughing at his comic fall. Once again, the classification is objective in that mistakes are possible. What is pain? Following from the chair example, any definition would have to include the idea that pain should be avoided, because that is why we classify things as painful.

The Naturalistic Fallacy is a Fallacy

The naturalistic fallacy asserts that it is impossible to derive a normative statement from a set of descriptive statements. It claims that 'is' statements cannot imply an 'ought' statement. Many philosophers think that it is a fallacy to attempt to derive an 'ought' from an 'is.' This is sometimes called the 'is/ought' gap.

This position implies that there can be no empirical evidence for a normative statement. Ultimately, the 'is/ought' gap implies that what we take as empirical evidence for a value judgment itself requires another value judgment. Deciding what will count as empirical evidence to support any value judgment will itself be a value judgment. For example, suppose that a film made us laugh and kept us engrossed for two hours. If we want to claim that this is evidence for the evaluation that the film was good, we have to make an additional evaluation that a funny and engrossing film is a good film. Furthermore, if we want to give empirical evidence for this second evaluation, then we shall have to presuppose another evaluation, such as 'Laughter is good.' In other words, an evaluative conclusion will only follow from a descriptive or factual premise given another evaluative premise. If the 'is/ought' gap thesis is true, then no set of purely descriptive statements by themselves can ever entail, or serve as evidence for, an evaluative judgment (Hare, 1965).

This means that there will be some basic value judgments, which do not have empirical evidential support. It implies that, if you make the basic evaluative judgment 'Pain is bad' and I affirm that pain is good then, there can be no reason to believe I am mistaken in any way, so long as I am consistent in all the value judgments I make. At root, it means that value judgments cannot be mistaken in the sense of being contrary to empirical evidence.

However, against this position, if proposition 2 ('Pain is non-conclusively and intrinsically bad') is an a priori truth, then there is no naturalistic fallacy. If 2 is an a priori truth then, what causes pain is instrumentally and non-conclusively bad and we can have evidence that something is bad, namely that it is painful.

The naturalistic fallacy a mistake because, as we have seen, it confuses conclusive and non-conclusive 'ought' statements. We can see this in two steps.

a) We *can* derive non-conclusive 'ought' from some descriptive 'is' statements. Necessarily, there is a non-conclusive reason to avoid pain. Similarly, there is a reason to respect the autonomy of another person. The gap is not between 'is' and non-conclusive 'ought' statements.

b) Rather there is a gap between 'is' and conclusive 'ought' statements. Given that something is painful, you cannot infer that there is a conclusive reason to avoid it. This is because the conclusive-reason statement requires that, all things considered, there is no other action for which there would be a better reason. There might be a good reason to endure the pain. No finite set of descriptive statements can rule that possibility out. Because of this, there is a gap between 'is' statements and conclusive 'ought' claims.

Because it fails to distinguish conclusive and non-conclusive 'ought' claims, the naturalistic fallacy is itself a fallacy. Furthermore, this failure to separate the two kinds of 'ought' statements leads to a mistaken diagnosis of the gap. Philosophers who think there is a naturalistic fallacy argue that this is because of a gap between facts and values. This cannot be right. Paragraph a) above shows this. Factual statements can imply evaluative claims. Paragraph b) provides an alternative diagnosis. Conclusive-reason statements require us to pick out the best action in the circumstances, amongst all possible actions, all things considered. They require a totality. No finite collection of descriptive 'is' statements can provide this totality. In a sense, the gap is between the finite and the infinite and not between facts and values.

From Pain to Morals

Suppose that 2 is an analytic a priori truth. A utilitarian could use this point to define what kind of evidence is relevant to establish a claim about what is morally wrong. To see how to generate morally normative claims, consider the following argument:

2. Pain is non-conclusively and intrinsically bad
3. An action that has bad effects is non-conclusively morally wrong
4. <u>Action A causes pain.</u>
5. Therefore, action A is non-conclusively morally wrong.

This argument shows one might derive a moral statement from a normative claim, i.e. 2. According to the utilitarian, premise 3 provides a sufficient condition for an action being (non-conclusively) morally wrong. As such, it too would an a priori claim. Premise 4 is an empirical claim. Therefore, tentatively, we can conclude that moral judgments involve both a priori and empirical components. The a priori claims state the criteria for an action being wrong, and the empirical claims state the relevant empirical facts. There is, however, an important qualification. None of this implies that utilitarianism is true. I have not affirmed that it provides necessary and sufficient conditions for morality, but rather, I have used it as an illustration of how a moral statement can have both a priori and empirical elements.

11
Appendix 1
Critical Reasoning:
Growing your own Teacher

Philosophy requires critical thinking skills that almost everyone can acquire with practice. It is a question of carefully and actively using one's attention. Guiding one's attention is the key to reasoning, reading and writing, but our attention is governed not only by the intellect, but also by our feelings. Hence, philosophy is a personal struggle, requiring the development of attitudes as well as skills.

The aim of critical reasoning is to think. It is never enough to merely consult one's opinions. The fact that one likes a view does not show it to be true or reasonable. Exercising one's intelligence is not a question of merely appealing to one's own opinions, or to any authority. The aim is to gain greater independence and strength of mind. Your teacher can impart information to you in the classroom, but you cannot miniaturize your teacher, and put him or her in your pocket for out-of class consultations. Therefore, you need to grow your own teacher. How to do this? Let us see.

A. Attitudes

Attitudes are very important part of our intelligence. If you are not open, you will not hear. If you are not critical, you will not ask. If you are not patient, you will give up. And if you cannot be simple, you will tie yourself in knots. This is not a complete list, but let us look at each attitude in turn.

1) Being open:

If we are attached to our beliefs, as if they were parts of ourselves, then we cannot appreciate other peoples' points of view. Furthermore, when we are closed, we cannot even understand properly our own beliefs. To appreciate the meaning of what you think, you have to understand what you are denying and why. Your comprehension of your own belief depends on your understanding of what those who disagree with you think.

Of course, if we are not open, we cannot hear what others say. If you feel: 'I have heard all this before' then, your ears will be closed and this is a loss. As an analogy, if each musician in a group had to listen individually to only one instrument of the orchestra, no one would identify the symphony as a whole. We need to hear the voice of others to be able to transcend our own limited perspective. Understanding requires the voice of others. Otherwise, we only hear ourselves playing our own instrument and never the full symphony.

We can embrace claims even when we think they are mistaken. Understanding involves far more than just identifying which statements are true and which are false. It requires appreciating the questions and seeing the overall map, rather than having answers. Embracing a view may require suspending judgment as to its veracity long enough to find out what is interesting and insightful about it. Don't ask too quickly 'Is it true?' but rather 'Have I understood it?' and 'What is good about this idea?' Criticism can come later.

However, being open is more than listening to people who disagree with you. It involves hearing voices that initially sound alien and learning to speak in new tongues.

There are three ways to help yourself be more open to the appreciation of a point of view opposite or different to your own.

- First, realize that your opinion is not *you*; your identity does not depend on what you think. You are a person and not a thought. Detach yourself from your beliefs. One way to do this is to realize that beliefs aim at truth and that the truth of your beliefs does not depend on your holding them.

- Second, embrace other views; look for the jewels of wisdom and make them your own; if necessary, suspend judgment.

- Third, allow yourself to think: 'Although I think this is true, it could be a mistake.' The thought 'This could be mistaken' can create a huge space in our feelings and minds.

2. Being critical:

We must not be satisfied too readily with easy answers and superficial questions. Our minds must be open, but also sharp. To become sharp-minded, we try to develop critical skills and ask: 'Is it true?' 'Is it relevant?' and 'What is the argument?'

- Is it true?

Sometimes we feel that there is something wrong with a statement and we are not sure why. We smell a rotten fish. Hold on to this feeling. If you do not like a view, this is no argument against it, but it might be a sign of rotten fish. Hold on to the feeling. Try to articulate what is wrong, but remember: you might be mistaken.

The opposite extreme is when we find nothing wrong with any view. No alarm bells ring, and even contradictory claims seem correct. One remedy for this is to see that every view excludes and denies something. What does the author you are reading exclude? Asking this question will throw into sharper relief what the author is claiming, and may provoke you to challenge it.

- Is it relevant?

This is very important. Sometimes debates are quite irrelevant to the point at hand. For example, in Chapter 6, I claimed that the ontological debate between materialism and dualism is irrelevant to the question of how consciousness is possible. In Chapter 9, we saw that the debate about how much agreement and disagreement exists between different societies is irrelevant to cultural relativism.

It is easy to get side-tracked in smaller ways, both in discussion and your own thinking. First, we need to concentrate on what is important. Second, making the relevant connections means asking: 'Does this really logically follow from that?' 'Are these two statements really contradictory?'

- What is the argument?

An author puts forward a theory. What reason is there to accept it, unless there is an argument or evidence in favor of it? None. At least, there should be a defense of it against objections. This means that, in reading, we must seek out the arguments and evaluate them. In discussion, we must ask for the arguments. For how to identify, construct and evaluate an argument, see Appendix 2.

Self-directed criticism:

Some people find it very difficult to be critical of their own views. To think, you need to have two voices inside you. One states and articulates what you believe, and the other throws a critical eye over what the first voice says. If you find it difficult to be skeptical about your own views, then practice thinking in the second voice. Ask yourself: 'What is the strongest argument that my opponent would give against my own claims?' 'How would he or she reply?'

Other people have the opposite problem. For them, it is so difficult to not doubt what they think that they hardly dare think anything, let alone speak. In this case, the second voice blocks the first. This may be due to a very strong fear of being mistaken, or to a feeling of insecurity. This does not mean that the second voice must be gagged. It just means that it must be disciplined. Ask it to stop bothering you while you are thinking in the first voice. Tell it that it can do its work later. Give the first voice space. Then let the second have its turn later.

3. Being patient:

Philosophy starts either when you get a fly in your brain, or you see a flickering candle. A fly in the brain is a question that will not go away. A candle is like an insight that comes and goes, and never quite illuminates the darkness totally. It flickers on and off. Flies and candles are frustrating. However, they motivate us to find answers. It is easy to squash a fly and blow out a candle. Once this happens, the quest for better understanding is dead. Both need to be nurtured by patience.

It is a common experience in philosophy to think you have the answer, and then discover that you do not. This is frustrating, but it is a good sign. You have made progress because your understanding is deeper. Moreover, you showed creativity in finding an answer and open-mindedness is rejecting it. Realizing this helps feed patience.

The lack of patience makes us go too quickly. For example, it can make us leap over stage 2 and go straight for the answer. Does God exist? Yes. Where has that answer got you? Nowhere, because on its own it means very little. Understanding requires analysis. Lack of patience makes us forget this.

Patient analysis helps us develop a third thinking voice: the strategist, who listens carefully to the other two voices arguing back and forth, and who directs where the discussion should go. The strategist sees forward, avoids dead-ends, and steers the argument towards key points. We need the third voice in thinking, reading and writing, and it is the fruit of patience.

Of course, too much patience, at the wrong time, makes us feel bored, as if we are going in circles and getting nowhere. This too can lead us to give up. Your strategic third voice should help you get out of corners and avoid dead-ends. It should be asking: 'Is this line of thought I am following important and relevant?' If it is not, change direction.

4. Being Simple:

Philosophy can be very complicated. Thus, it is good to be simple. Simplicity can be like an axe, cutting through tangles and knots. It requires being able to concentrate on what is important. It requires being able to express a point clearly and concisely.

An enemy of simplicity is hesitation. If you are not sure what you want to say, or think it is mistaken, then you may try to hedge by adding in lots of qualifications. This is a symptom of over-anxiety about being mistaken. It is better to affirm what you have to say simply. You can always add in the qualifications later.

Other enemies of simplicity are unnecessary technical vocabulary and too many long sentences. (But don't tell Kant that!) If you have lots of ideas crowding in, better to separate them, and deal with them one at a time. If you are using technical philosophical words, such as 'ontological,' be sure that you explain them simply.

One aid to simplicity is the example. A good example makes the point obvious, without introducing irrelevant complications. It helps your reader and you.

Conclusion:

Cultivating the attitudes needed to think well is a vital part of doing philosophy. Those attitudes help us nurture the skills we need. Without them, the skills are like tools that we do not know how to use.

B. Some Skills

Attitudes express themselves in the management of skills. Here are some of the skills that we need to develop and which will be presented in the other appendices.

- Finding and constructing an argument
- Critically assessing an argument
- Analyzing claims
- Reading philosophy
- Writing a paper

The final point: the heart of philosophy consists in shaping one's mind, not in filling it with facts. The process is more important than the information.

12

Appendix 2: Applying Logic

The beauty of argument is that it enables us to keep from accepting rubbish. It is more than just an intellectual tool, because it is also an attitude, namely that of wanting to find the support or argument for a claim, and to examine it carefully and fairly. The aim of this appendix is in no way to explain even elementary formal logical theory, which basically consists of constructing formal systems to represent certain logical inferences. Instead, the aim is to outline some of the most basic uses of simple logic, especially the syllogism.

First, here are a few simple tools. An argument is a chain of reasoning designed to prove a conclusion. It consists of two parts: the premises and the conclusion. In the following simple argument, 1 and 2 are the premises, and 3 is the conclusion that they logically entail:

ARGUMENT A

1. All dogs are animals.
2. <u>Fido is a dog.</u>
3. Therefore, Fido is an animal.

This is a logical or valid argument. An argument is logically valid if and only if the conclusion follows logically from the premises. 'Follows logically' means that if the premises are true then the conclusion must also be true. Or, put another way: in a valid argument, it is impossible for the conclusion to be false and the premises true. You cannot accept the premises and deny the conclusion. That would be a contradiction.

This does not mean that the premises of a valid argument are true. In argument A, if we replace the name 'Fido' with the name 'John' in 2 and 3, we will still have a logically valid argument, even though premise 2 will now be false, because John is not a dog.

Please be careful: the expressions 'valid' and 'invalid' apply only to whole arguments. They do not apply to premises or conclusions on their own, that is to individual sentences. This is because the term 'valid' applies to the connection between the premises and the conclusion in an argument. It concerns the argument as a whole, specifically whether the conclusion follows logically from the premises. Consequently, an argument can be valid even if the premises are false. Individual premises and conclusions are sentences that are either true or false, but not valid or invalid. In other words, do not confuse valid/invalid with true/false.

To help you see this difference, consider the following. A valid argument can have false premises. For example:

ARGUMENT B

1. All fish have lungs.
2. All daffodils are fish.
3. Therefore, all daffodils have lungs.

This is a logically valid argument because the conclusion does follow logically from the premises, even though the two premises and the conclusion are false. When we ask whether an argument is valid, we are NOT asking whether the premises and conclusion are true.

Consider also the following: an invalid argument can have a true conclusion and true premises. For example:

ARGUMENT C

1. The moon is smaller than the earth.
2. Mars is smaller than Jupiter.
3. Therefore, Pluto is smaller than Neptune.

This argument is not valid because the conclusion does not follow logically from the premises, even though the premises and conclusion are true.

Ultimately, we are looking for arguments that are sound. An argument is sound if and only if it is both logically valid and it has true premises. Given that an argument is sound, then the conclusion must be true.

This is the minimum amount of theory we need in order to begin the application. To think properly using these tools, you have to be able to do three things.

1. First, you will have to take a piece of text and convert it into a logically valid argument in syllogistic form, such as arguments A and B above.
2. Second, after that you must learn how to critically assess an argument.
3. Third, you need to learn how to construct our own arguments.

1) Converting Text into Argument

Suppose that you have a piece of polemic text that argues for a conclusion. The first thing you have to do is find the conclusion. Identify as carefully as you can what the author is arguing for. Write it down. Expressions such as 'hence,' 'therefore,' 'thus,' and 'it follows that' usually introduce conclusions.

The next task is to find one of the premises. Expressions, such as 'since,' 'because,' 'in view of,' and 'as shown by,' usually introduce premises.

Now you can begin to lay out the argument as a syllogism. Perhaps, the text has one or more premises missing. You will have to work out what these are. In any case, it is worth seeing if the author has actually stated all the premises sufficient to logically imply the conclusion. You should try to make the argument logically valid.

2) Evaluating an Argument

Now you have an argument to evaluate. Given that it has been constructed in a logically valid form, one only has to ask: 'Are the premises true?' Focus on each premise in turn, asking whether it is true, probably true, or probably false, or simply false. In other words, ask yourself: 'Is the premise true?' of each premise in turn.

Here is a simple point to improve. Many students, when raising an objection to an argument, complete only 80% of the work and leave the final 20% unfinished. For example, as a criticism of the second premise of the cosmological argument, they might affirm: 'It is possible that there was no first event at all' (see page 18). The problem is that, at the last moment, when one is supposed to finish the deal and clinch the point, they fail to bring closure to the objection. You have to complete the job, for example, by asserting: 'Therefore, premise two is false and this argument does not prove the existence of God.' You have to relate your objection back to a specific premise of the argument to make it stick.

In examining an argument, do not evaluate the conclusion. That would be like ignoring the argument itself. To see why, we have to distinguish two tasks. The first is evaluating an argument, and the second, criticizing a position. For example, showing that an argument for the existence of God is not sound is not at all the same as arguing in favor of the claim that God does not exist. Showing that the argument fails does not show that the position or conclusion itself is false.

Typically, television debates confuse the two. The first side gives an argument against, for example, the legality of abortion. The opponents present an argument in favor of the legality of abortion, ignoring the arguments of the first. In effect, the two sides are talking across each other, ignoring what the other says. It is like two monologues.

If someone presents an argument for a conclusion which you think is mistaken, please first address his or her argument. Having done this, you can present an argument for the opposite point of view. These two steps are equivalent to the two separate processes of evaluating an argument and criticizing a conclusion. One reason why some debates seem to go on forever is that people conflate these two processes.

Let me put the same point in another way. Of course, if an argument is valid and the premises are true, then the conclusion *must* be true. However, if an argument is valid and the premises are false, then the conclusion *need not be false*. In other words, you can have a logically valid argument with false premises, and a true conclusion. A valid argument with false premises just provides no proof or evidence for the conclusion. For example:

ARGUMENT D

1. All women have beards.
2. Lenin is a woman.
3. Therefore, Lenin has a beard.

In summary, we have to ask two questions about any argument:

a) Is the argument logically valid?
b) Are the premises true?

151

If the answer to both is 'Yes,' then the argument is sound and the conclusion is true. If the answer to at least one of these questions is 'No,' then the argument does not provide any reason for believing the conclusion. However, this does not mean that the conclusion is false.

3) Constructing an Argument

The first two steps tell us what to do with someone else's arguments, such as the ones that we dig out of a book. But they do not tell us to construct our own arguments, which is a much harder task.

- First, you need to know what you are arguing for. Try to identify the conclusion. This is perhaps the hardest step because if you state the conclusion unclearly, it will be much harder to construct the rest of the argument.
- Second, usually, one of the premises is obvious.
- Third, you should write the argument down in logical form because, once you have identified one premise and the conclusion, you can work out what the other premise(s) must be.

The most common problem in constructing one's own argument is to avoid begging the question. One cannot assume that the conclusion is true when framing the premises. When constructing a valid argument, think of what you must do as follows: Take two ideas and put them together. Each one of them on its own is not a sufficient for the conclusion, but together they are. As an analogy, think of an argument as a cake. You need the flour, the sugar, the milk and the eggs. You can bake a cake only when you have all those ingredients and none of them on their own is sufficient to make a cake. You only obtain a conclusion by mixing together the ingredients, or the independent premises. Furthermore, if you try to make a cake out of an already existing cake, you have not made one at all. Similarly, if you assume what you are trying to prove, you do not have an argument.

Sometimes, none of these tips work. They do not make the argument clear. Alternatively, the argument looks artificial and unconvincing. In which case, try writing down your original idea as clearly as you can without constructing it in a logical form. Then, treat your text as if it were someone else's: Follow the steps you would follow in such a case. If that does not work, rewrite your piece and try again.

A. Valid Forms Based on the Connectives

Let us look very briefly at a little more of the theory of logic. What makes an argument valid? It is the form of the sentences concerned, not what they actually assert. Some arguments are based on the logical connectives between sentences, which are:

| and | & | not | ~ |
| if...then..$\supset$ | | either ...or... | v |

For example, '$p \supset q$' means 'if p then q' or 'if 'p' is true then 'q' is true.' Also, 'p & $\sim q$' stands for 'p and not q.' The letters 'p' and 'q' stand for any well-formed sentence. The three most common argument forms based on the connectives are:

1. Modus Ponens	2.Modus Tollens	3.Disjunctive Syllogism
If p then q	If p then q	Either p or q
p	Not q	Not p
———	———	———
Therefore, q	Therefore, not q	Therefore, q

Using the above symbolism, these arguments can be put into logical form as follows:

1. $((p \supset q) \& p) \supset q$
2. $((p \supset q) \& \sim q) \supset \sim p$
3. $((p \vee q) \& \sim p) \supset q$

B. Valid Forms Based on Set Membership

A set is a collection of entities. For example, Hilary Clinton is a member of the set of all women, which is a more formal way of expressing the claim 'Hilary Clinton is a woman.' The members of a set are said to belong to that set. For example, 'All As are B' means that all members of the set of A things belong to the set of things that are B. An instance of 'All As are B' is 'All apples are fruit' or 'all members of the set of apples are members of, or belong to, the set of all fruit. Some valid argument forms based on set membership are:

All As are B	No B is A	All As are C
No C is B	Some C is A	Some Bs are A
———	———	———
No C is A	Some Cs are not B	Some Bs are C

C. Some Formal Fallacies

The following argument forms, based on the connectives, are logically invalid, and are among the so-called formal fallacies.

1. The fallacy of affirming the consequent:
   If p then q; q; therefore p

2. The fallacy of denying the antecedent:
   If p then q; not p; therefore not q

In 'If p then q,' 'p' is the antecedent and 'q' is the consequent.

D. Some Informal Fallacies

1. The fallacy of equivocation: using a single word in more than one sense. For example, matter is divisible; the mind is indivisible; therefore, the mind is not made of matter (see page 62).

2. The fallacy of begging the issue: implicitly using your conclusion as a premise. For example, the universe must have a cause; God caused the universe; therefore, God exists (see page 19).

3. Ad hominem: attacking the person, rather than arguing against the claim made by him or her. For example, anyone who denies the existence of God wants to undermine morality.

4. Ad ignoratiam: (appeal to ignorance) arguing that a claim is true just because it has not shown to be false. For example, all the arguments for the existence of God fail; therefore, God does not exist.

5. A false dichotomy: claiming that there are only two mutually exclusive options when, in fact, there are more options, or the two options are not mutually exclusive. For example, either this is a fact or it is merely an opinion (see page 116).

6. Arguing against a straw man: setting up your opponent's position so that it appears weaker than it really is. For example, the materialist claims that the mind is the brain (see page 67).

13

Appendix 3:
Analysis

Analysis is a vital part of thinking. As we saw in Chapter 1, it can be foolish to go directly from question to answer, because that means accepting the question as it was given to us. Furthermore, understanding does not just consist in having answers, because you have to know their meaning and worth.

Analysis is an attempt to understand better the meaning of what we think. Different types of philosophy involve varying methods of analysis. Some philosophers claim that analysis consists in revealing the true logical form of a statement. Others claim that it consists in breaking down complex ideas into their simple components. Others that it involves showing how words are used in the contexts of ordinary conversation. Others affirm that it requires explaining the original meaning of words or their etymology. According to others, analysis should reveal the cultural and historical presuppositions of what we assert.

We do not need to wed ourselves to any particular method of analysis, or to bother arguing which is superior. All of them can be useful, and there are no rules determining when best to use one method as opposed to another. It is best to think of analysis in terms of what it must do for us: either it must help us to ask better questions, or it must help us find better answers. Either it feeds back into stage one, or directs us forward to stage three.

There are two reasons for analysis.

- One is to gain insight by understanding more deeply the meaning and significance of what it said or asked.

- The second is to spot and avoid mistakes.

The guidelines outlined below can be applied to both aims. We can analyze what others write, but also what we ourselves think. We can analyze both questions and replies. The points I will make about statements can be applied also to questions.

1. Is the question or statement clear?
2. What are the key terms, and what do they mean?
3. Are there important distinctions to be made?
4. Are there any hidden assumptions?
5. Are the logical consequences plausible?

1. Clarity: Questions and Statements

Let us start with questions. Analyzing a question requires replying to the following: 'Why are we asking the question anyway?' 'Why is the question important?' and 'What hangs on the answer?' Knowing why we are asking helps us to grasp what would count as a good answer.

Typically, when a person has a philosophical puzzle on the brain, many questions come to mind. In which case, it is important to select the best of the various formulations of the question that occur to one. A confused question will yield a confused answer. Try not to ask too many questions at once, because that is a sure recipe for chaos and bafflement.

Is the statement or question clear? Here are some ways in which a statement can be unclear.

- It can contain ambiguous or vague words. For instance, the expression 'objective' has many uses. If someone wants to defend or attack the objectivity of science, this key term must be clear.

- Is the statement logically complete? Statements can be incomplete, such as 'Your mother is taller' or 'This is better.' One needs to answer the questions: 'Taller than who?' and 'Better than what, and in what ways?' The problem is that the incompleteness of a sentence can be hidden. For example, the claim 'Her approach is more efficient than his' may sound complete, but efficiency is always relative to an end and, consequently, one must specify the relevant end. Another example is the phrase 'For the sake of freedom,' which is also incomplete because it fails to answer the question 'Free from what?' Yet another example is the sentence 'Moral claims are relative.' This too is incomplete, because it fails to specify what they are relative to.

- Is the statement a priori or empirical? It is possible to confuse the two. For example, 'Where does morality come from?' sounds like an empirical question regarding the origin of a thing. However, morality is not an object, and, perhaps, the question really means: 'How can we justify moral judgments?' If this is so, then it is a priori.

- Is the question or statement normative or factual? 'All people are born equal' sounds like a factual claim but, in reality, it means something like 'All people should be treated equally,' which is normative claim. Another example is 'We need a definition,' which probably means 'We need a good definition' and as such, it is normative.

2. Key Terms

- What are the key terms?
  Try to identify which words are doing the work in a sentence. For example, in the question 'What is the meaning of life?' the key word is 'meaning.' Does it mean 'purpose?' Or, does it mean 'intrinsic value?' Or, perhaps, the idea is that a life is like a story.

- What do the key words mean?
  Once identified, the key words need explanation. We want to gain insight into how they function. Often, important words have several meanings and distinguishing these helps us to be

158

clearer. There are several ways to analyze key terms. These include the following.

1. Definitions

One way to specify meaning is with an adequate definition. Definitions are often given by specifying necessary and sufficient conditions.

- Sufficient conditions: (e.g. having a husband is a sufficient condition for being married). If S is a sufficient condition for A, then the following conditional statement will be true: if S then A.

- Necessary conditions: (e.g. oxygen is a necessary condition for being a living animal) If N is a necessary condition for A, then the following conditional statement will be true: if A then N.

Not all terms can be given such a definition. Some terms are too vague or too metaphorical for such a precise analysis. In which case, we need alternative ways to explain how they function.

2. Essential contrasts

Another way to dig deeper into the meaning of a key term is to think of the contrasts that it plays on. For example, 'free' is usually opposed to 'obstacle,' or 'forced to.' For example, 'need' should be contrasted with both 'desire' and 'luxury.' Such contrasts show us how an expression works. How does the contrast function? For example, what makes something a luxury? By answering this, we can better grasp the term 'need.' When and how does the essential contrast break down?

As the above example show, all terms work by exclusion. So, one way to be clearer about a key term is to think of what it excludes. If it is not apparent what the expression excludes, then probably the term itself is not clear either.

3. Paradigm examples

You want to understand the expression 'success,' which is a powerful but unclear word. One way to do this is to think of model or uncontestable examples of success, and try to explain what makes them such clear examples. By doing this, you can give important criteria for success and this would constitute a good step forward in the analysis of the term.

4. Logical form

However, thinking about 'success' or 'freedom' is not likely to get us very far. The problem is that the two terms are nouns and it appears that they refer to a thing. It is more illuminating to analyze the corresponding adjectives 'successful' and 'free' because what counts as a successful person would not be the same as what counts as a successful action or metaphor. Being clear about the correct logical form of a word is another important step in analysis.

5. Dictionary definitions

Never simply copy the dictionary to give you a philosophical definition. Typically, dictionaries only report how a word is actually employed in ordinary usage, without trying to clarify or improve on that usage. It does not tell us how a word *should* be used. Nevertheless, dictionaries can help us gain insight, and so can a thesaurus and the origin of a word.

3. Important Distinctions

One way to analyze a statement is to draw an important distinction. For example, in Chapter 6, we distinguished the statements: 'The mind is the brain,' 'mental states are brain states,' and, 'the having of mental states is identical to the having of mental states.' This was important because only the last claim was plausible (see page 68). For example, in Chapter 9, we distinguished two senses of the phrase 'What is right in one culture might be wrong in another.' Failure to draw this distinction makes cultural relativism appear more plausible than it really is (see page 110).

4. Identifying Hidden Assumptions

Words, questions, statements and whole theories can have hidden assumptions and much philosophy consists in unearthing these. We have seen that this is an important process regarding questions. 'Have you stopped beating your mother yet?' 'What is *the* meaning of life? 'What is the point of human existence?' All of these questions make assumptions that may be false, and questions that involve a false presupposition are best not answered. Most philosophy is an attempt to reply to conceptual questions and, therefore, we need to analyze the question, to see if it involves false presuppositions.

Theories too contain assumptions. Sometimes, two opposing points of view or theories can be shown to be both incorrect because they share a fundamental assumption. Kant, for example, argued that empiricism and rationalism have in common a false assumption, namely that there is only source of knowledge, either the senses or reason. In Chapter 10, we showed that the conflict between utilitarianism and Kantian moral theory rests on a false assumption: namely that moral actions must be defined completely in terms of rules (see page 137). There was also an underlying hidden false assumption in Chapter 6 concerning the conflict between dualism and materialism, namely that the nature consciousness is primarily an ontological issue (see page 70).

For both questions and theories, one very common form of mistaken assumption is the false dichotomy. This occurs when a theory or question only offers you two alternatives, when in fact there are others. For example, in the philosophy of mind, such a false dichotomy is the claim that either dualism is true or else reductive materialism is. This false dichotomy makes dualism appear more attractive than it is (see page 86).

Even the use of individual words can involve a false assumption. In Chapter 3, when discussing 'nelephant,' 'God' and 'exists,' we saw that words themselves can have built-in assumptions or limitations (see page 34). When we transgress those limitations, we are in danger of using the word without sense.

5. Are the Logical Consequences Plausible?

Suppose that your favorite philosopher draws a conclusion. One way to analyze that conclusion is to ask whether it has true or plausible implications. Put yourself in the shoes of someone who thinks that your favored thinker is usually mistaken. This will help you attend to the implausible elements of what he or she says. If P implies Q and Q is false, then we can conclude that P is false too. This argument form is called Modus Tollens (see page 153). For example, if dualism has the implication that animals are not conscious, and animals can be conscious, then this means that dualism is false. If utilitarianism has the implication that we should hang the innocent man to prevent the riot, when we should not do so, then this implies that utilitarianism is false.

Counter-Examples

Because thinkers are concerned with conceptual or non-empirical questions, this means that they are interested in defining or explaining important concepts or words. One way to challenge a definition is to think of a counter-example: an example that shows the definition to be mistaken or incomplete. For instance, if I define 'justice' as an equal distribution of something good, you can think of two types of counter-example to this definition:

- One is an example of a situation that is just but is not equal. For example, suppose that Mary and Martha each have two mangos. Mary sells hers for $10 and with the money buys eggs, which she later sells for $30. Martha eats one of her mangos and sells the other for $5. The situation at the end of the day is that Mary has $30 and Martha has $5. The situation may be just without being equal.
- The second is an instance of a situation that is equal but is not just. For example, as a diabetic, John needs two capsules of insulin, but Henry needs none. Henry and John each have only one capsule. This situation is equal, but it may not be just.

Generally, if a thinker defines J as X, then we can try to think of two kinds of counter-examples. These are examples of J that are not X, and of X that are not Js.

14

Appendix 4:
Making Books Sing

The root of many of our problems with reading is that, after grade school, we automatically assume that we can read. However, this is misleading because the process of learning to read never finishes. What we learned at grade school was how to convert marks on a piece of paper into sounds, but that is only the very first step in the process of reading. Reading is the art of understanding what is written.

Many people feel that books are dead. However, if one knows how to read, one can make the written word sing. Imagine you can invite the most interesting people in the history of humanity into your living room and converse with them. Well, in effect, you *can*, by reading their books. However, this requires knowing how to make those books alive by making them speak to you and discovering the life in them.

Reading too fast kills a book. At school, many of us were encouraged to read quickly. However, if one rushes through the chapter, one is unlikely to be able to answer the question: What were the main conclusions of what you read?

The Song in the Head Phenomenon

You will have experienced this phenomenon. You hear a song on the radio that you like and, during the day, the song continues to sound in your head. As a result, you think that you know the song. After all, it is inside you, and it sounds right. However, if you try to sing it out loud, you may learn the painful truth, namely that you do not know the tune and that you remember only a tiny part of the lyrics. You did not know the song at all well, even though you felt as if you did.

There is a similar phenomenon regarding silent reading. The reading sounds right in your head, and you feel as if you are gliding along, comprehending everything you read. However, when you try to actually sing it aloud, you cannot do it. In other words, if you were asked searching but simple questions about what you have read silently to yourself, you may be unable to answer them. For this reason, I recommend that one should read out loud, especially difficult or important passages.

When you read out loud, you can give the sentences their proper intonation and emphasis, especially if you do not read fast. When you read to yourself silently and rapidly, you lose the possibility of hearing the tone of the author. What you read converts itself into your own voice. Out loud, you can read the text with life. It helps to imagine that it is the author speaking to you.

Maps: Getting in the Helicopter

Last night, in preparation for class, your teacher read a chapter of a difficult book. The next day, he or she comes to class and tells you what its conclusions and arguments are. What is the good of that? The information may be useful, but what is much more important is whether you can do what your teacher has done: understand a difficult passage of a work sufficiently well to be able to explain it to other people in your own words. This capacity is what should concern us. The teacher's brain is much the same as anyone else's and this means that almost anyone can do what he or she did, given adequate training and practice. By doing this for the class, he or she has deprived you and your classmates of the opportunity of practicing such abilities.

We tend to read like ants, getting caught up in the details of each sentence and failing to see the pattern of the chapter as a whole. Understanding a chapter well requires reading from a helicopter's perspective and giving up the ant's viewpoint. From a helicopter, one can see the contours of a chapter and take it in as a whole.

To help us adopt the helicopter's perspective, we need to draw a map of the chapter we are reading. Drawing a map of a chapter is quite different from making a summary or a resume, because a map concentrates more on the structure or lay-out of the chapter, without delving too much into the details of what is being said.

The way to draw a map is to look for the important transitions in the chapter. For example, suppose that the author begins his or her chapter by explaining why the problem he or she will address is important. When she has finished doing that, she explains the thesis that he or she is going to argue for. That is the first transition. Next, suppose that she is going to tell you what other people have said about this thesis, and why they are mistaken. That is another transition. The next transition might be that he or she states the argument for the thesis or conclusion. After that, he or she might defend those arguments against apparently strong objections. Finally, he or she might show the important implications of the position.

We can put of all of these transitions together to make a map of the chapter. If it is yours, mark the book to show where the transitions are. The important clue to look out for is not what the author is saying, but rather what he or she is trying to do. Ask: 'What is the author trying to achieve?' Possible answers include the following: introduce the theme, give an argument, clarify his or her position, answer objections, and illustrate the importance of a point. To draw a map, you need to discover where he or she finishes doing one thing and starts doing another. To do this, for example, look for how many arguments the author advances in favor of his or her position, how many objections he or she replies to, and where each one begins and ends. Such points define the structure or topography of the chapter. Once one does that, one already has the helicopter perspective of the work.

Sometimes, we can easily discover such structural features of the text, because the author actually tells us what they are. Such points can be called signposts. They are invaluable, because they save you, the reader, work. For example, if the author writes 'There are four objections that we need to consider,' look for the four objections and number them by the side of the text. These form part of the structure of the chapter. Many authors divide their chapters into sections and even sub-sections; these too are invaluable in constructing the map.

Signposts often occur near the very beginning of a chapter or a section. Occasionally, they can be found at the end of the work too. Remember that on such occasions, the author steps out of the text, just to help you with guidelines. You should reply: 'Thank you, author, for the help; I have not ignored you.' Sometimes, authors actually make the map for you. For example, towards the beginning of a chapter, they might write: 'In this chapter, we shall examine the positions, evaluate each one and show that none are viable.' This is gold dust. Pay attention; they are trying to save you work.

The map you draw of a chapter is important. Without it, you probably have not understood the work because you have got lost in the details. With a map, if you do become lost then, at least, you can identify where this happened and how the point fits into the whole. You may even be able to tell whether it is an important point.

There may be many different correct ways to map out a chapter, but this does not mean that you cannot make mistakes in drawing your map. In any case, the map should not be too complicated and detailed, because the point is to help you achieve an overall vision of the structure.

Do not start making your map until after you have read the chapter through once at a normal speed (which means not too fast). While rereading the chapter, draw your map on a piece of paper. Afterwards, you can reread the chapter more slowly for a third time, knowing fully where you are. One advantage of this method is that if you do get lost then, at least, you know where this happened. For example, you will know that you could not understand the reply to the third objection. Furthermore, you will get a feel of whether the difficult point is really vital to your overall grasp of the chapter.

The map itself is very useful, but, even more important is that you have undergone the process and acquired the skill of mapping out a chapter for yourself. If someone else had done it for you, you would have lost the opportunity to train your attention in the right way.

The Radio Test

Sometimes, after reading a chapter, many people cannot articulate what the main point was. For example, they cannot specify whether the author was for or against capital punishment. They may think that the author was obscure, but probably it was the reader who was vague. Most authors have a specific point to make, which is why they bother to write their work in the first place.

The remedy for this is the radio test. Imagine that you have just read a chapter by Peter Singer on euthanasia in his book *Practical Ethics* and you happen to visit a public radio station precisely at the time when this is the theme of their program. The presenter of show asks you to explain in a few sentences what Singer said in his chapter on euthanasia. You have thirty seconds. You can't waffle, because there are a million people listening to you. You have to be crisp, concise, and straight to the point, for example as follows: 'Singer's main point is that... His argument for that is... In answer to the objection that... he would reply...'

Please don't tell your audience what Singer's chapter was about. For instance, don't list topics in the following way: 'First, Singer discusses the different types of euthanasia; afterwards, he looks at the social effects of euthanasia, and so on.' Instead, tell them what Singer actually asserts or concludes. Don't report, for example: 'Singer considers the question of euthanasia and examines the difference between active and passive euthanasia.' Instead, assert he following: 'Singer thinks that euthanasia is justified only when.... ' 'His main argument is...' 'He claims that there is no intrinsic difference between active and passive euthanasia because...'

Are you ready to practice the radio test in your room, in the bath, or with your friends? Please keep practicing it with all discursive texts that you read. Here are some ways to help you pass the radio test.

- First, find the main conclusion or point of the chapter or section
- Second, look for the main arguments in favor of or defending that conclusion.
- Third, search for the main implications or important consequences of the conclusion.

The three-fold structure, conclusion, arguments, and implications, fits many works of philosophy quite well, but certainly not all.

Inner Noise

Sometimes it is possible to completely misunderstand what an author writes because one reads the author as affirming what one wants him or her to say. In other words, one's own ideas and wishes get in the way. If you have a strong opinion on the topic you are reading, be careful of doing this. Let the author speak to you first in his or her voice. While doing this, try to put your own views to one side. Later, you can use the force of your own view to critically evaluate what she has said. In other words, try to separate the two processes: taking in what the other person says, and critically evaluating it.

A less extreme version of the same phenomena is when you read a passage, and it sparks off lots of ideas. If while you are reading, you have lots of thoughts, then it is best to jot them down on a piece of paper. You can return to them later, after you have finished reading.

Reading, listening, thinking and writing are beneficial skills and arts to be cultivated. By working to improve your reading skills, you will strengthen your thought processes. It is largely a question of attention and of actively trying to understand, rather than passively taking the words in.

Summary

Read each selection/chapter at least twice: once, to get a general understanding of the work, and again, more carefully, to understand it more deeply, taking notes and drawing a map. Don't read too fast and, if the passage is difficult, try reading aloud, as if the writer were speaking to you. To avoid becoming lost in long sentences or complex thoughts, you can do three things:

First, identify the main simple point that the author is making in the chapter. Try to answer the question: 'What is the author's main point or conclusion?' to yourself *aloud* in a verbal 1/2 - 1 minute summary, and then in writing, in 3 or 4 sentences. This is the radio test. If necessary, try also doing the same for paragraphs or subsections.

Second, authors give us maps, signposts, and clues, and you must look out for these. For example:

- Often towards the beginning of a chapter, the author will tell you what she plans to achieve in a chapter and how. He or she will outline the road-plan. Pay attention to this; it's like a map of the chapter.
- Usually the first sentence of every paragraph tells you what the author is going to do in that paragraph. She will tell you the purpose of the paragraph, such as to state the problem, or to give definitions, distinctions, arguments and conclusions. Pay attention to these signpost sentences, and then you will understand better how the paragraph or section fits into the whole. Without that understanding, you will easily get lost.
- Look out too for phrases such as 'the essential point is' or 'what I'm trying to say is,' and for places where the author repeats him or herself carefully; usually these are clues that he or she is making an important point.

Third, look out for the relevance of other things the author says to the main point. If you understand the central point of a chapter and see how the other things the author says are relevant to that point, then you will not get lost. Furthermore, you will remember the piece much more easily. Usually, the best way to grasp the relevance of minor points is to understand what the author is trying to do. For example, he or she may be trying to qualify the central point, explain some of its implications, or distinguish it from some other superficially similar point. Often, the main point an author is trying to make is some principle, and much of the rest of what he or she says can seem either as an argument for that principle, or as drawing out its implications. Look out for conclusions, arguments and implications.

15

Appendix 5:
Tips for Writing an Essay

There are many kinds of papers, for example, ones that explain the position of an author, and those that compare two authors on a specific theme. However, you can also write your own philosophy. Since this is the most challenging kind of paper, we will concentrate on it.

Writing is a form of thinking. It requires you to be clear and to the point. It is a good way for you to test and improve your thinking skills. However, to serve as such, it must be also an exercise in communication. In writing, you are not merely expressing your ideas because you are writing to someone, for an audience who will read it. You make an idea clearer to yourself by making it clearer for others.

Step 1: Choosing

You need to decide what to write about. Suppose that you have free choice. In which case, choose the topic or area that most interests you. However, defining a topic is not enough. It is an invitation to ramble. You need to select a specific question concerning that topic. Your paper basically will be an answer to that question. Having a question gives direction, aim, and organization to your work. It is important to select a question that interests you, which is strategically important, and which is specific enough for you to answer.

In this first step, be careful to select a philosophical or non-empirical question. Otherwise, you will engage in empirical speculation rather than philosophy. For example, 'How did humanity develop its concept of morality?' is an empirical question, which requires an empirical investigation of history, and cultural anthropology. Without empirical data, an answer would be merely speculation. It would be more appropriate to ask a conceptual or philosophical question, such as 'What is morality? or 'How can moral judgments be justified?"

Also, be careful to choose a question that is both not too vague and not too broad. Choose a question which you can answer, and for which you can justify your answer with arguments. Don't try to solve everything in one paper.

Step 2: Preparation

Your work will consist in your answering your question, and justifying your answer or the thesis with arguments. However, your thesis can be negative, such as 'The standard answers to this question are all flawed,' or 'So and so's argument for X is not sound.'

1) Preparation
It is important to jot down all your ideas on a separate piece of paper and, then, try to put them in some order of importance. Afterwards, try to structure the most important points into a paper framework. In other words, draw a preliminary map of the paper you are going to write. Later, you can develop this rough map into a more structured plan.

2) Research and background reading
It is also important to read and research. You are going to develop your own position, but this does not mean that you cannot use the work of other philosophers. There is no need to reinvent the wheel. However, it is important to not be side-tracked by your reading; consequently,

- Stick to points that are directly relevant to your plan; do not get distracted into other issues. Keep it simple. However, use the work of authors who disagree with you in order to understand the strongest objections to your own claims.

- Too much reading can be a way or an excuse to avoid writing. Budget your time.

- Try to select books that are directly useful to your task. One way to do this is to look at the table of contents and the index and to browse, before deciding to read relevant chapters. However, a book that is not directly relevant may have a useful bibliography.

- In selecting books, be practical. Use books that will help you, rather than ones that complicate the issue. Usually, on most themes, there are introductory survey books that can give an overall view of an area. On the whole, more recent books of this type tend to be more useful than older ones. Try to find out what the most important recent books on your question are, and then select. In other words, choose methodically.

- Only use the directly relevant sections from your sources. You may not need to read the whole book. Use the table of contents and the introduction, where the author usually reveals his or her plan for the book as a whole, chapter by chapter.

- Always cite your sources in a footnote. When you disagree with an author, you must explain exactly how and why. Never simply list the views of other philosophers and then add your own 'opinion' at the end. Everything you write you must believe, even when you are debating a point with another author.

3) Plan
Before you begin to write your essay, you should plan it. Convert your rough map into a more developed plan. Here are some important points:
- Start with an introduction; end with a conclusion.
- To be interesting, a paper needs tension. For example, you can contrast two views, and argue in favor of one of them. Furthermore, our own thinking also needs this kind of tension, because understanding your own view requires contrasting it with what you are denying.
- Structure your paper well. Make your points paragraph by paragraph, one by one, sequentially and in logical order. For example, never critically assess a position without first explaining it.
- Remember stage 2 of philosophy. The key words in a question often require explanation and analysis. There may be important distinctions to make.
- State your main thesis as clearly as you can. You can explain by showing what it is meant to deny and by distinguishing it from other similar claims. An example would have the following form: 'In affirming P, I mean to deny Q because...'

and 'In asserting P, I do not mean to argue for R, with which P may be confused.'

- It is usually important to explain the importance of your main thesis and to motivate the question that your paper will address.
- Try to anticipate objections to your position and respond to them. It is important to make the objections to your own position as strong as you can. A poor paper is invariably one that makes the objections and opposing positions weaker than they really are.
- Distinguish between evaluating an argument and a position. It is one thing to show that an argument in favor of euthanasia is not sound; it is another to show the position itself is false.

There is no single correct plan for a paper. But in the absence of anything better, the following might be used:

1. Outline the problem and why it is important
2. Explain how theory A tries to solve the problem
3. Give the main or strongest argument in favor of theory A
4. Critically evaluate the argument
5. Give the strongest argument against theory A
6. Critically evaluate the argument
7. Draw your conclusion.

Step 4: Writing

As you write, you will probably see points that you did not plan for. This is normal, but it should not serve as an excuse for hopping around. Always be relevant and sequential. Do not write stray thoughts, however interesting, into the middle of a paragraph. Jot them down on a separate piece of paper, and later, work them into the appropriate paragraph. If need be, you change your plan, but don't abandon it.

You are writing for an audience. Help them understand what you want to say. Each paragraph should have one main point. The point of the next paragraph should be relevant to the one before. Connect them. Don't link two paragraphs with vague transitions, such as 'This brings me to another point.' Your reader will not see the connection.

If you write long sentences, this may be a useful sign that you are not making the connections between points explicit enough. Long sentences usually contain too many thoughts and qualifications. They are complicated. Furthermore, people write long sentences usually because they have ideas while they are writing. Write your new ideas somewhere else. Stick to the original point of your sentence, without distraction. Furthermore, your new ideas may have valuable insights. In which case, they need space to be developed, perhaps in a separate paragraph. They will not be clear if they are squeezed in among other points.

Usually, in a philosophy paper, it is best to avoid being impressionistic too often. Do not tell your reader how you feel. Try to argue the case instead. The main point of your paper is to explain and defend a thesis or claim that answers a specific question.

Suppose that you get stuck and that you can find no words to put down on paper. This may be a sign that you are subconsciously criticizing what you want to say before you have had a chance to express it. If nothing feels right, decide to put the critical side of your brain in low gear. Let what you want to say come out, however imperfectly. You can use your critical voice later to improve your work.

Step 5: Re-reading and Re-writing

You may think that you have finished writing your paper, but probably you have not. An essential part of writing is rereading and redrafting what you have written. Do not hand in a first draft. Most authors have to rewrite and rewrite and rewrite.

When you reread your paper, do so out-loud, as if you were someone else. In this way, you can hear it as an outsider would. It is better to be your own critic than to let your reader do it. In this way, you can strengthen your own thinking processes and write a better paper. Furthermore, to be your own critic, you have to pretend to be reading someone else's work. To keep the flow of your reading, you can mark passages that need changing and come back to them later.

You should reread your paper for two types of change. First, for the sake of altering the details and of improving your writing style. Perhaps, there are words you can cut out, or sentences you can simplify. Perhaps, there are points that are not clear enough. Perhaps, you need a good example. Second, rereading the paper is a way to check the fundamentals of your idea. Good luck!

16
Bibliography

Adams, Douglas, *Hitch-Hiker's Guide to the Galaxy*, Harmony
    Books, 1989
Armstrong, David, *The Materialist Theory of Mind*, Routledge,
    1968
Alston, W.P., 'The Inductive Argument from Evil and the Human
    Cognitive Condition', in *Philosophical Perspectives*, Vol.
    5, ed. J. Tomberlin, Ridgeview, 1991
Audi, Robert, The Cambridge Dictionary of Philosophy,
    Cambridge, 1996
Bennett, J., *Locke, Berkeley, Hume*, Clarendon Press, 1979
Berkeley, G, *Berkeley's Philosophical Writings*, ed. Armstrong,
    Collier Books, 1965
Churchland, Paul, *Matter and Consciousness*, MIT Press, 1988
Davidson, Donald, 'Mental Events,' *Actions and Events*, Oxford
    University Press, 1980
Descartes, R., *Discourse On the Method*, (ed. Anscombe and
    Geach, Nelson, 1954
Descartes, *Meditations*, ed. Anscombe and Geach, Nelson, 1954
Harris, John, 'The Survival Lottery,' *Philosophy*, 1975
Hare, Richard, *Freedom and Reason*, Clarendon Press, 1965.
Hick, John, *Evil and the Love of God*, Harper and Row, 1977
Hick, John, *Disputed Questions*, Macmillan, 1993
Jenkins, J., *Understanding Locke*, Edinburgh University, 1983
Kant, I., *The Critique of Pure Reason*, Macmillan, 1929
Kant, I., *Groundwork of the Metaphysics of Morals*, Translated by
    H.J.Paton, Harper, 1956

Kant, I, *The Critique of Judgment,* Clarendon Press, 1988

Kim, Jaegwon, *Philosophy of Mind*, Westview Press, 1996

Kolak, D., *Wittgenstein's Tractatus*, Mayfield, 1998

Layton, Bentley, *The Gnostic Scriptures*, Doubleday, 1987

Locke, John, *An Essay Concerning Human Understanding*, Oxford, 1978

Macaró, Juan, trans., *The Upanishads*, Penguin, 1965

Mill, J.S., *Utilitarianism*, London, 1873

Morris, Richard, *The Edges of Science*, Prentice Hall, 1990

Nagel, E., *The Structure of Science*, Harcourt Brace, 1961,

Nagel, Thomas, 'What is it like to be a bat?' in *Mortal Questions*, Cambridge University Press, 1979

Nozick, Robert, *Philosophical Explanations*, Belknap Press, 1981

Poundstone, W., *Labyrinths of Reason*, Doubleday, 1988

Rachels, J., *The Elements of Moral Philosophy*, McGraw Hill, 1999

Rawls, John, *A Theory of Justice*, Harvard, 1971

Ryle, Gilbert, *The Concept of Mind*, Barnes and Noble, 1949

Sacks, Oliver, *The Man who Mistook his Wife for a Hat*, Picador, 1985

Searle, John, *The Rediscovery of the Mind*, MIT Press, 1994

Smart J.J.C., and Williams, B., *For and Against Utilitarianism*, Cambridge University Press, 1973

Smart, Ninian, *The Philosophy of Religion*, Oxford University Press, 1979

Spinoza, B, *Ethics*, Dover, 1955

Stich, S., *From Folk Psychology to Cognitive Science*, MIT Press, 1983

Swinburne, Richard, 'The Problem of Evil,' *Reason and Religion*, ed. Stuart Brown, Cornell University Press, 1977

Thomson, Garrett, 'The Strong, the Mild and the Weak: Readings of Kant's ontology,' *Ratio*, Dec. 1992

Thomson, Garrett, *On Kant*, Wadsworth, 2000

Thomson, Garrett, *On Descartes*, Wadsworth, 2000

Thomson, Garrett, *On Locke*, Wadsworth, 2001 (a)

Thomson, *Bacon to Kant*, Waveland Press, 2001 (b)

Wittgenstein, L., *Tractatus Logico-Philosophicus*, see Kolak 1998

Wittgenstein, L., *Philosophical Investigations*, Blackwell, 1953

Williams, Bernard, 'A Critique of Utilitarianism,' in *For and Against Utilitarianism*, J.J.C. Smart and B. Williams, Cambridge University Press, 1973

Williams, Bernard, *Descartes: The Project of Pure Enquiry*, Penguin, 1978